Thinking about
Cultural Resource Management

Heritage Resources Management Series

Series editor: Don Fowler, University of Nevada, Reno
Sponsored by the Heritage Resources Management Program
Division of Continuing Education, University of Nevada, Reno

Books in this series are practical guides designed to help those who work in cultural resources management, environmental management, heritage preservation, and related subjects. Based on a series of successful workshops sponsored by the University of Nevada, Reno, the books are designed to be "workshops between book covers" on important strategic, legal, and practical issues faced by those who work in this field. Books are replete with examples, checklists, worksheets, and worldly advice offered by experienced practitioners in the field. Future titles in this series will deal with assessing historical significance, management of archaeological sites, working with native communities, and other topics.

Volumes in the series:

1. *Cultural Resource Laws and Practice: An Introductory Guide,* Thomas F. King (1998)

2. *Federal Planning and Historic Places: The Section 106 Process,* Thomas F. King (2000)

3. *Assessing Site Significance: A Guide for Archaeologists and Historians,* Donald L. Hardesty and Barbara J. Little (2000)

4. *Tribal Cultural Resource Management: The Full Circle to Stewardship,* by Darby C. Stapp and Michael S. Burney (2002)

5. *Thinking about Cultural Resource Management: Essays from the Edge,* by Thomas F. King (2002)

Thinking about Cultural Resource Management
Essays from the Edge

Thomas F. King

A Division of Rowman & Littlefield Publishers, Inc.
Walnut Creek • Lanham • New York • Oxford

PRESS

A Division of Rowman & Littlefield Publishers, Inc.
1630 North Main Street, #367
Walnut Creek, CA 94596
www.altamirapress.com

Rowman & Littlefield Publishers, Inc.
A Member of the Rowman & Littlefield Publishing Group
4720 Boston Way
Lanham, MD 20706

12 Hid's Copse Road
Cumnor Hill, Oxford OX2 9JJ, England

British Library Cataloguing in Publication Information Available

Library of Congress Cataloging-in-Publication Data

King, Thomas F.
  Thinking about cultural resource management: essays from the edge / Thomas F. King.
  p. cm.
Includes bibliographical references and index.
  ISBN 0-7591-0213-9—ISBN 0-7591-0214-7 (pbk.)
  1. Historic preservation—United States. 2. Historic sites—Conservation and restoration—United States. 3. Historic buildings—Conservation and restoration—United States. 4. Architecture—Conservation and restoration—United States. 5. Cultural property—Protection—United States. 6. United States—Cultural policy. 7. United States—Antiquities—Collection and preservation. I. Title
  E159 .K57 2002
  363.6'9'0973—dc21   2002002181

Printed in the United States of America

♾ ™The paper used in this publication meets the minimum requirements of American National Standard for Information Sciences—Permanence of Paper for Printed Library Materials, ANSI/NISO Z39.48—1992.

If a writer doesn't generate hostility, he is dead.—V. S. Naipaul

Cartoon by Nicholas Del Cioppo

To the memory of Janet Friedman, who didn't always agree, but always encouraged

Contents

Acknowledgments

Innumerable people have contributed to the chapters that make up this book. Some have given me ideas that I've shamelessly adopted and adapted; others have challenged me to think up solutions to problems, and others have irritated me to a point at which I could not resist the impulse to sit down and put fingers to keyboard. I am grateful to all, and will not even try to name them. I do, however, express particular thanks to those who have taken part in the classes I teach for the National Preservation Institute, those who have invited me to take part in symposia that required the preparation of papers, and those who take part in the vigorous discussions that enliven ACRA-L, the Internet forum maintained by the American Cultural Resource Association.

And as always, I'm grateful to Mitch Allen and his colleagues at AltaMira Press for encouraging me to pull this book together, for patiently and sympathetically awaiting its completion, and for absorbing my abuse.

T. F. King
Silver Spring, Maryland

Foreword

In the editor's introduction to Tom King's (1998) *Cultural Resource Laws and Practice,* I wrote that over the many years I have known Tom, he has remained "dedicated, acerbic, articulate, eminently rational, and at the same time passionate about issues that matter." Further, I opined that "he has come to understand, as well as or better than anyone in the country, the nuances, limits, and meanings of laws and related rules which inform cultural resource management practice." Both statements are still true, in my opinion. In the present volume, however, he has achieved a new status, that of Chief CRM Curmudgeon, a title I bestow with great respect. Dictionary definitions of *curmudgeon* contain such adjectives as "surly," "bad-tempered," "irritable," "cantankerous," etc. However, dictionaries cannot, and do not, convey the true essence of curmudgeonhood: One who is rational in the Renaissance rather than the Enlightenment sense, that is, one who thinks that *humanitas* is central to being human and interpreting what that means; one who thinks outside the box; one who cares enough to give us his/her very best thoughts on matters of significance and importance. That those very best thoughts often go against the grain of received "wisdom," or current practice, and hence get branded as "cantankerous," is a flaw in human understanding, not the state of curmudgeonhood. Because such thoughts cast new light, or make us uncomfortable, it is all the more important that they be carefully considered; "taken into [serious] account," as it says in Section 106.

You don't have to agree, but you should thoughtfully consider the lines of argument and their implications. If you do, you'll invariably learn something useful.

In these essays, Tom seeks, as he says, "a cultural resource management that reflects and respects the cultural values of living peoples"—all living peoples; not just one or another special interest group, descendant communities, ethnic groups, habitues of megacorporations, or bureaucrats, but all of us. His message is that because we usually focus on the "letter" of the CRM laws and regulations, rather than the spirit—the *humanitas*—thereof, we unnecessarily weave tangled webs and often lose, mar, or deface that which we seek to preserve, to cherish. Tom's essays are about spirit, *humanitas,* not bureaucratic procedures; about people, not about rote rule following. There is much in these essays of great value for everyone, practitioner or interested party, in the conservation, preservation, and appreciation of the multiple heritages extant in our society. Would that all concerned parties heed what is being said; we would be the richer for it.

Don Fowler
April 22, 2002

Introduction: Thinking about Cultural Resource Management

In 1989 I resigned my position at the Advisory Council on Historic Preservation[1] and hence lost the security of federal retirement benefits. An unanticipated consequence of this self-created bar to retirement has been that although I have not yet *outlived* many other people who have been with "cultural resource management" (CRM)[2] in and around the U.S. government since the field's inception, I have survived many of them in active practice.

The fact that I have actually been in CRM practice (depending on what one considers CRM) for something between thirty-five and forty-two years is a little startling to me. At various times over those decades I have been a teenage "pothunter,"[3] a field archeologist, a federal bureaucrat, an official-of-sorts in a territorial government's "state" historic preservation program, an administrator of statewide and academic contract archeology offices, and a private consultant, teacher, and writer of regulations, guidelines, and policy. Not unexpectedly, during this lengthy and checkered career I have developed quite a number of opinions about how CRM should be done and what's wrong with the way it actually is done in the United States and elsewhere. I've propounded these opinions in books, published articles, conference papers, and speeches, and in the last few years on the Internet, usually provoking massive silence in response.

Undaunted, early in 2001 I began to toy with the idea of pulling together a few of my "old" papers and writing some others anew, to present some of the notions that I still feel are worthy of consideration by my peers and successors in the CRM enterprise. Rather to my surprise, when I mentioned this idea to my friend and long-suffering publisher, Mitch Allen, he said he thought that some people might actually *pay* for a volume comprising such papers and that AltaMira Press would be interested in publishing it. Thus this book was born.

It's my immodest belief that I exercise a degree of critical creativity in my CRM practice. This is not to say that all my ideas are good, or even that they make sense, and it's certainly not to say that they're popular, but I like to think that at least they provoke thought. So it's my hope that some of the essays that follow will encourage people—especially younger people now entering the field or evolving as leaders in CRM—to think creatively about their practice, to explore new approaches, to be open to innovation.

As I've worked on these essays, I've come to realize that they—and a lot of my other writings, my teaching, and my consulting work in CRM—reflect an assumption about the field's purpose that isn't necessarily shared by all its practitioners. I might as well 'fess up to it at the outset: I think that CRM is about finding solutions to human problems through human interaction.

Not all human problems, of course; CRM won't provide a cure for AIDS or deflect asteroid strikes, control global warming, or (very often) feed the hungry. But the central problem with which CRM practitioners grapple is a very human one—how to hold on to what people value about the cultural past and present (which is often the natural world as well) while getting on with the future. Inevitably, this involves a struggle for balance in which moral imperatives are not particularly clear-cut—however much many of CRMs practitioners and critics would like them to be.

I don't think it's a sin to destroy an old building, or even (though it's a lot more difficult for me) a cemetery, or even (harder still) some aspect of a living culture. Okay, maybe that's going too far; construction of the Three Gorges Dam is a sin, as is rewarding its builders with the right to host the Olympics. But I digress. Generally speaking, I don't think that most CRM conflicts have clear right/wrong, good/bad answers. The whole business is a matter of finding balance between conflicting but legitimate human values.

A bit farther outside the mainstream—at least outside mainstream practice, if not rhetoric—I believe that CRM is about what *people*—plain old people-in-the-street people—value, as well as about what professional archeologists, architectural historians, and their ilk value. Rhetorically, the leadership of organizations like the National Trust for Historic Preservation in the United States makes much of its appeal to the grass roots. When push comes to shove, however, what organizations like the Trust really pay attention to are things that some official—in our country the Secretary of the Interior through the Keeper of the National Register, or an official local historic preservation body—designates as significant. In contrast, I really don't care what the Keeper or my local landmarks board thinks is important—except that as people their views should be every bit as important as those of the guy who picks up my trash every Thursday. I think it's outrageous to extend consideration in planning only to places that the Keeper or the local board is willing to admit to an official list. I think it's elitist, antidemocratic, and contrary to what CRM really ought to be about.

And finally, I think good CRM is about people with conflicting views sitting down and reasoning with each other, seeking mutually agreeable solutions. The consultation process that's at the core of the regulatory scheme set up under Section 106 of the National Historic Preservation Act[4] should be central to all types of CRM, and it should be a real, open consultation process in which all concerned parties can freely participate. The lack of such a process, I think, is one of the great weaknesses of the National Environmental Policy Act (NEPA) and other environmental and cultural resources laws. The evolution of the Section 106 consultation process over the last decade toward ever-increasing structure and exclusiveness makes me sad.

But in recognizing these assumptions in the way I approach CRM, which form the rationale for many of the arguments made in the following essays, it has also slowly dawned on me that there is not a CRM law in this nation, or probably in the world, that is explicitly based on them. I suppose that should daunt me, but it doesn't; it just makes me wonder why Congress has never written such a law. Why it never provided, for example, for mandatory, nonbinding consultation among all concerned with the environmental impacts of federal actions. We have public hearings, sure, and everyone knows what shams they usually are; we have comments on environmental impact statements, which consultants get paid good money to absorb and sweep under the rug; but we do not have a process of reasoning together to seek agreement on balanced solutions. Except under Section 106, of course, but even there consultation isn't very explicit in the law, and it's focused on the narrow question of how to deal with historic properties—defined as things the Keeper, directly or indirectly, sees as important. It's odd.

I began work pulling these essays together in the spring of 2001. The job was nearing completion when we in the United States experienced the horror to which we have come to refer, self-protectively, simply as "September 11." Such an event inevitably induces a response in any thoughtful person. Not only the desire to go kick the kidneys out of some terrorists, but the desire to understand why it happened, and continues to happen. And anyone with some sense for history, which inevitably breeds suspicion for the premise that it's all about unmitigated evil in cosmic struggle with perfect good, has to reflect on how we Americans could be so hated that people who clearly are not (all, at least) mere madmen could feel justified in doing such things to us. One naturally goes on, being unable to do much else about the situation, to wonder what one personally has done, or may be doing, or may do in the future, to either contribute to the hatred or reduce it. In my case, all this impelled me to read a book—Mark Juergensmeyer's excellent study of religious terrorism *Terror in the Mind of God.*[5] Some of Juergensmeyer's conclusions bring me back to CRM and (a source of some self-satisfaction) give comfort to my biases.

Among the causes that Juergensmeyer adduces for religious terrorism is the sense, on the part of its perpetrators and supporters, that their cultural and spiritual roots are being ripped out by the forces of secular modernity, as represented by economic globalism and the pervasive influence of "American culture" in international contexts and "liberal government" in the domestic arena. Marginalized and unable to protect what they value through the political process or by other peaceful means, a small percentage of people turn to violence.

> Perpetrating acts of terrorism is one of several ways to symbolically express power over oppressive forces and regain some nobility in the perpetrator's personal life. Those who have been part of cultures of violence

and who have participated in acts of empowerment—even vicariously—
have experienced the exuberance of the hope that the tide of history will
eventually turn their way. . . . Alas, the experience has often been fleet-
ing. Sadder still, it has been purchased at an awful cost.[6]

It would be the height of hubris for me to suggest that cultural resources management is going to do much to defuse international terrorism, and I don't. But each of us can try to contribute as best she or he can
to a world in which people (or at least people who aren't nutcases) don't
feel compelled to be terrorists. Those of us in CRM can, I think, make
some small contribution to such a world. Unfortunately, we can also contribute in our own small ways to perpetuating the attitudes and institutions that can drive people and groups to despair and that occasionally but
disastrously lead to violent acts of defiance. When we accept and respect
the legitimacy of a small group's cultural values—whether the group is
made up of American Indians, cattle ranchers in Montana, or Southern
Baptists, and try to work with such groups to maintain the integrity of
their cultures and communities in the face of assault by the forces of
modernity, we're contributing in some tiny way to their ability to work
peacefully and productively with other parts of society. When we ignore
such values, or insist on their expression only in terms with which the
dominant culture is comfortable, we fuel frustration and anger. In the little corner of the world that is CRM practice, I believe that we contribute
to a better world by trying to make government actions responsive to the
cultural values and concerns of local communities of all kinds, by respecting their values and making as sure as we can that they're listened to by
those in power. I think we do quite the opposite when, for instance, we
ignore elements of culture that don't quite mesh with our own professional interests in archeology or history or ethnography, when we exclude
such elements from consideration in planning based on nitpicky interpretations of regulatory criteria or strict legalistic distinctions between the sacred and the secular, and when we pretend that community concerns can
be adequately addressed via government-run public hearings and unilat-
eral decisions by government officials.

I suppose I can be accused of trying to harness the self-reflective
energy generated by September 11 to pull my own wagon, or to validate
my own existence. Maybe so; maybe it's my own way of getting past the

marginalization that almost all of us feel in the wake of the attack. On the other hand, I'm not saying anything that the last several generations of applied anthropologists haven't said, over and over—that it's vitally important to pay attention to people's cultural values, that these values should be respected, not only because if we don't, people may rise up and smite us, and not only because it preserves the interest and vibrancy of the world, but simply because it's the right thing to do. But the fact that it makes me feel a little better, and the fact that it's all old news, doesn't make it less true. Culture really does matter, and there's real danger in failing to pay attention to it. Those of us who appropriate the word "cultural" to name our field of practice have a special obligation, I think, to help government and industry understand and respect the world's real cultural resources—the things that people in communities believe in and value.

Before We Begin . . .

Each chapter in this book was written at a particular time, often for a particular audience. As a result their tones vary, and they assume different levels and kinds of understanding of CRM on the part of their readers. Generally, I assume that a reader will have read one or more of my textbooks on CRM subjects and/or have a good deal of background experience or education in the field. Inevitably, though, some readers will have more familiarity with some aspects of CRM than with others—just as I do, of course. It would be burdensome and redundant to try to provide a serious overview of the contexts in which the parts of this book were written, but we have included, at the end of the volume, a brief glossary of some obscure but commonly used terms and acronyms that appear in the following chapters.

This book is divided into four parts. Part I is made up of five chapters on relatively general matters, all reflecting the notion that CRM is not about the practice of particular disciplines, be they archeology or history or the fine assembly of National Register nominations. Part II comprises eight chapters dealing with various aspects of impact assessment—the heart of CRM practice in the United States, however little some practitioners like to admit it. Part III has four chapters about "indigenous issues"—CRM matters of concern to American Indian tribes and other indigenous people, and part IV contains three chapters dealing with aspects of my own natal discipline, archeology. A concluding chapter is an act of unmitigated conceit, suggesting how CRM should be structured not only in the United States but also in the European Union and, by implication, in the galaxy generally.

Notes

1. A small U.S. government agency that advises the president and Congress on historic preservation matters and oversees the "Section 106 Process" that provides review of federal, federally assisted, and federally licensed actions to control their effects on historic properties.

2. See King 1998a for a lengthy discussion of the various definitions of CRM.

3. A term used in the United States for nonprofessional collectors of Indian artifacts, even where pots are not the objects of the hunt.

4. As articulated, today in a very confusing, user-unfriendly way, in regulation at 36 CFR 800 (ACHP 2000).

5. Juergensmeyer 2000.

6. Juergensmeyer 2000:185–86.

Part I

Thinking about Cultural Resource Management as an Extradisciplinary Enterprise

The term "cultural resource management" was dreamed up by archeologists, and in many institutions and agencies, CRM continues to be thought of as largely an archeological enterprise.[1] Other disciplines have involved themselves in the management of cultural resources, and impacts on such resources, under other rubrics—"historic preservation" for architectural historians and historical architects, "public history" among historians, "social impact assessment" among anthropologists and sociologists. But archeologists and historians do historic preservation, and social impact assessment assumes and often reveals the importance of cultural factors in the lives of communities and in their relationships to the impactable environment. Practitioners of other disciplines—landscape history and architecture, planning, law, engineering, geomorphology, geography—also do cultural resource management, either explicitly or under other rubrics. It's a mixed-up field.

Which is, perhaps, as it must be, at least at this stage in CRM's evolution. There is no one discipline that routinely concerns itself with, and teaches its students about, the full range of cultural resources—cultural landscapes, archeological sites, historical records, social institutions, expressive culture, old buildings, religious beliefs and practices, industrial heritage, folklife, artifacts, spiritual places. Nor is there any whose self-identified practitioners regularly think about how to manage all such resources, or to address impacts on them. CRM necessarily involves multiple disciplines.

In the regulations implementing the National Environmental Policy Act (NEPA), the Council on Environmental Quality (CEQ) called for NEPA analyses to be "interdisciplinary"—that is, to involve practitioners of all disciplines pertinent to a resource or impact working together in productive synergy.[2] CRM is likewise thought of (sometimes) as an interdisciplinary enterprise.[3] Unfortunately, few NEPA analyses, and few exercises in CRM under whatever legal authority, are truly interdisciplinary. Most are at best multidisciplinary—with various experts working independently, the results of their work merely compiled.

In truth, though, even if practice *were* interdisciplinary it wouldn't be enough. Practice in CRM can't be limited—shouldn't be limited, at least—to practitioners of established scholarly disciplines. And it's not, except in the narrow minds of some authors of policy and guidelines. The mason who does a good job repointing a crumbling historic stone wall is managing a cultural resource. So is the househusband who organizes his neighborhood to stop demolition of a locally valued bridge, building, or landscape. So is the retired Marine colonel who researches her family history and archives the results. So is an elder in an Indian tribe or other indigenous group, with a high school education, who preserves and passes on his tribe's traditions. CRM should be, and in real-world terms is, more than interdisciplinary, it's *extradisciplinary*. It should involve the synergetic efforts of everybody who's relevant to and concerned about a cultural resource issue, whether they have professional credentials or not.

One of our serious challenges in CRM is to foster extradisciplinary practice, and it's often hard to do. When a government agency like the National Park Service (NPS) sets out to write regulations, standards, or guidelines for some CRM activity like the conduct of surveys or nominating places to the National Register of Historic Places, it typically and understandably assigns the writing to people with credentials in some presumably pertinent field—a Ph.D. in history, an M.A. in anthropology with an archeological focus, a degree in architectural history. The person assigned this responsibility cannot help but look at the world through the lens of the discipline in which he or she has been trained, and whatever direction he or she drafts reflects this viewpoint. The draft direction, whatever it is, typically is shared with practitioners of other disciplines, who may tinker with it to make sure that their own professional biases are properly represented but seldom do anything more—and are seldom equipped by training or interest to do more. The result is policy that reserves archeology to the archeologists, old buildings to the architectural historians and historical architects, living cultures to the ethnographers, and so on. Thus merely multidisciplinary practice becomes enshrined in official doctrine; the creativity and public responsibility that should result from synergetic extradisciplinary CRM is rigorously avoided. I think this is unfortunate.

The five chapters in this part of the book examine this problem from various perspectives and are the products of various times and contexts. The first is a presentation I made to archeologists and a few other anthropologists at the annual meeting of the American Anthropological Association in 1995, so it deals with the widespread view that archeologists have allowed to develop—indeed been instrumental in creating—that equates CRM with archeology. The second broadens the critique a bit to include ethnography, the subfield of anthropology that describes living cultures. More generally, though, it's about the dangers in letting CRM be defined by, and with reference to, academic disciplines of all kinds. Chapter 3 discusses one of the most backward, most narrow-minded of CRM's institutions, and of all such institutions the one most responsible for enforcing narrow disciplinarianism—the National Register of Historic Places. The fourth chapter presents a positive model for nonprofessional (hence extradisciplinary) public involvement in CRM's archeological aspects, in the work of Arkansas's Hester A. Davis. It also bemoans the fact that Hester's model is not widely emulated. The fifth and last chapter discusses what I think is the false dichotomy between "process" and "substance" in CRM and how the knee-jerk preference for the latter illustrates the need to get beyond disciplines in training CRM practitioners.

Notes

1. See King 1998b for a discussion of CRM's parentage and its unfortunate results.

2. 40 CFR 1502.6.

3. Oddly, however, I can find no official regulation or guideline, at least among those pertaining to the historic preservation side of CRM, that actually calls for interdisciplinary work.

1

*Doing a Job on Culture: Effective but Self-Serving Communication with One of Archeology's Publics**

A bunch of the boys were whooping it up
In the Denver Airport bar
As the snow piled high,
And the planes wouldn't fly,
In the winter of 'Seventy-Four.

The talk turned 'round, as it often did then,
To the new thing they called "preservation."
But like the relations
Of our exhumations,
Some of us had reservations.

"Old ladies in tennies!" we muttered and grumped;
"Don't want to be thought of like THEM!"
Then one of us brightened,
Said he: "Don't be frightened!
We'll call what we do CRM!"

CRM. Cultural Resource Management. What does it mean? What is this thing called CRM?

---

*Presented to a symposium on "communication with archaeology's publics" at the American Anthropological Association's Annual Meeting, November 1995.

Let's deconstruct the term. As anthropologists we all know what "cultural" means, right? Of or pertaining to culture, obviously, and although we may define "culture" in various ways depending on our theoretical bent, I think most of us would agree that culture—and any particular culture—is (in the words of the National Park Service), "a system of behaviors, values, ideologies, and social arrangements . . . (that) help humans interpret their universe as well as deal with features of their environments, natural and social."[1]

"Resource" has a pretty clear definition in my Webster's as "something that lies ready for use or can be drawn upon for aid." Something that's certainly or possibly useful to someone, in other words.

"Management" is defined, of course, as "the act or art of managing;" and to "manage" is to "direct or conduct affairs, to carry on concerns or business."

So, "cultural resource management" must mean "the direction or conduct of affairs pertinent to things of possible use in systems of behaviors, values, ideologies, and social arrangements by which humans interpret the universe and deal with their environments."

But wait, some of you may say, that's not what *we* mean by *CRM*. CRM is understood by academic departments across the country as—in the words of a recent SAA Bulletin article—"the care and feeding of archeologists."[2] It means applied archeological research, under a bunch of obscure federal laws. It means performing surveys to identify sites that may be eligible for the National Register of Historic Places, testing them for evaluation, and sometimes excavating them before they're destroyed by federal projects. That's what CRM is to most archeologists, and it's defined pretty much the same way by many federal agencies. Why is this?

This brings us back to my bit of doggerel. The term *CRM* was dreamed up, to the best of my perhaps faulty recollection, by a group of archeologists, snowbound at the Denver airport in 1974, en route home from a rather informal conference.[3] The conference had been called to consider how archeology was responding and could respond more advantageously to the rapidly developing corpus of environmental and historic preservation laws and regulations—the National Environmental Policy Act (NEPA), Section 106 of the National Historic Preservation Act, Executive Order 11593, the new Section 106 guidelines of the Advisory Council on Historic Preservation, and the very recently enacted

"Moss-Bennett Act." The term was invented because nobody wanted to be lumped in with the "historic preservationists," who were, we felt, largely ignorant of archeology in general and prehistory in particular, besides mostly being blue-haired little ladies who tut-tutted over their sherry about the demolition of old buildings. At the time, "natural resource management" was being much discussed in the federal land managing agencies, some of whom were just awakening to their responsibilities as stewards of the nation's wildlands, so it was natural that we archeologists created a parallel term for what we did—or rather, for what we wanted to do—for the same agencies in the cultural sphere.

The modest point I want to make in this paper is this: Archeology has done a very good job of selling "cultural resource management" to a very important public—the agencies that are required to manage their impacts on the environment under NEPA, Section 106, and a variety of other statutes. However, in doing so without thinking through what we meant by CRM, and what others might take the term to mean—and by failing to think through our own responsibilities as anthropologists, we have allowed—even encouraged—those same agencies to ignore the impacts of their actions on a vast array of cultural resources that do not happen to fit comfortably into our archeocentric definition.

To avoid seeming to have created too much of a straw man, I'll acknowledge that the definition of CRM has broadened a little since the mid-1970s. To broader-minded practitioners, CRM embraces not only aspects of archeology and such allied disciplines as geomorphology, but also the applied practice of historical research, architectural history and historical architecture, sometimes landscape architecture, sometimes a bit of urban planning. Sometimes CRM is understood to require a bit of ethnography, in order to identify traditional cultural places that may be eligible for the National Register of Historic Places, and occasionally it may embrace a bit of folklife documentation, vaguely justified as a means of "salvaging" information about a community's associations with the landscape that some agency intends to muck up.

What CRM is *not* taken to embrace, I suggest, is the bulk of what this nation's diverse cultural systems value most and most regret and resist losing into the great American melting pot—the social institutions, beliefs, and lifeways that give each such system its unique identity.

Some examples:

- the importance of open space to a Navajo and the need for propinquity to relatives in a Pueblo community;

- the ideology of nonmechanical farming among Amish agriculturists;

- the value of natural quiet to Native American vision seekers;

- the role of early morning markets in the life of an urban Chinatown and that of coffeehouses in a Middle Eastern community;

- the place of wild rice harvesting in the self-identity of a Native American community in Wisconsin, and the value of high steel work to certain Mohawk groups;

- a western cowboy community's perceptions of its relations with the land;

- the practice of traditional basketmaking and the plant resources it requires;

- the land-use ethics of ranchers and miners in Nye County, Nevada.

These are all certainly "cultural resources," if we follow the dictionary definitions of its constituent words, but they have little if anything to do with properties eligible for the National Register of Historic Places, and still less to do with archeology. Sometimes we can construct a connection with the National Register, true. Sometimes the Native American subsistence practices, or the needs of the basketmakers, will give sufficient significance to a particular place on the landscape that we can justify it as Register-eligible. But it's a stretch, and often an impossible one, if it's relevant at all. On the whole, CRM as archeologists have defined it simply doesn't reach these kinds of resources.

Well, I hear practitioners grumbling, "That's not our fault." The law doesn't require consideration of things like land-use ethics and traditional subsistence. It only requires consideration of places that are eligible for the National Register.

Wrong. That's what *Section 106* requires, but that's only one piece of one federal law.

What do you think is required in order to:

- assure for all Americans safe, healthful, productive, and esthetically and culturally pleasing surroundings?

or to:

- preserve important historic, cultural, and natural aspects of our national heritage?
or to:

- wherever possible, (preserve) an environment that supports diversity and variety of individual choice?

Those are from the National Environmental Policy Act (NEPA)[4]—the umbrella under which all Federal agencies carry out the bulk of their environmental planning activities. Considering impacts on historic properties under Section 106 is one of the activities that shelters under the NEPA umbrella, but it is only one. There's lots of room to consider effects on other cultural resource types under NEPA, to say nothing of such laws as the American Indian Religious Freedom Act, which relates to a specific kind of resource—Native American religious practices—that has only marginal connections with the National Register of Historic Places.

But on the whole, impacts on cultural resource types other than places eligible for the National Register are not addressed under the NEPA umbrella. They're not addressed, in substantial measure, because archeologists have hogged the umbrella's shelter.

In 1994 I oversaw a study for CEHP, Inc., under contract with the Council on Environmental Quality (CEQ), examining how "cultural resources" are dealt with in NEPA analyses.[5] We examined sixty-nine final environmental impact statements (EISs) filed during 1993 with the U.S. Environmental Protection Agency (EPA)—that's a sample of about 25 percent—against a series of preformulated hypotheses and test implications. We augmented this review by interviewing a range of experts in various aspects of environmental impact analysis and reviewing the pertinent literature. The study resulted in several findings, of which the following is most pertinent to the subject of this paper:

> The typical EIS addresses only two aspects of the cultural environment. Socioeconomics are routinely addressed, though the emphasis in most EISs is on the economic, with little attention to the social. "Cultural resources" are usually addressed as well, but this term is almost invariably taken to mean "historic properties" as defined in the National Historic Preservation Act (NHPA).
>
> Sixty of the sixty-nine EISs used the term "cultural resource," or words very close to it (e.g., "cultural values" or "archeological and cultural resources").
>
> In fifty-eight of the sixty cases, the way "cultural resource" was used made it clear that the writers equated it with "historic property" as defined in NHPA. Other aspects of the cultural environment tend to be addressed only in passing, if at all.
>
> Perhaps the most important thing that falls through the cracks between socioeconomics and historic properties is the way of life of the affected community, defined by such characteristics as subcultural variation, community stability and change, community values, the symbolic meaning given by the community to aspects of the environment, the basic self-perceived identity of the community, and the community's patterns of land tenure and land use (Freeman 1992).[6] Only three of the EISs we reviewed included references (typically vague and passing) to things like "lifestyles."

The long and the short of it is, we have very thoroughly communicated to federal agencies and environmental planners the need to address "cultural resources" as we define them, and the rest of culture is the victim of our success. Archeological resources are pretty routinely dealt with— under the "cultural resources" rubric—in federal agency planning, as are, most of the time, obvious historic architectural resources, but every *other* kind of cultural resource gets considered only to the extent it has fervent advocates who know how to play the cultural resources game well enough to overcome the opposition not only of the agency planners and decision makers but often of the agency "cultural resources managers" as well.

That can take considerable doing when it's the "cultural resources managers" who define how the game is played. An SHPO archeologist of my acquaintance, for example, has been agonizing over how closely you have to space shovel tests to define the boundaries of a sacred hill.

And Native American sacred sites get considered only because there are specific laws requiring it, and because of the infamous *National Register Bulletin* 38.[7] When it comes to non–Native Americans, and nonreligious cultural values, everybody's eyes glaze over. *Nobody* in CRM is concerned, for example, about the cultural resources interests of those folks in Nye County, Nevada, which is too bad, because their interests are as "cultural," and as legitimate, as anybody else's. And maybe if we'd paid attention to them all this time they'd see CRM as something that could help make sure that those terrible jackbooted fascist federales paid attention to their grassroots concerns, instead of categorizing archeologists among the oppressors. As anybody who's read *Time* magazine[8] lately knows, the chickens in Nye County are coming home to roost, in large numbers on the heads of archeologists—and having grown up on a chicken ranch I can assure you, that's not going to be pleasant.

I imagine I can hear some of you saying, "I don't care about the land-use ethics of Nye County, Nevada. The people who live there are a bunch of rednecks."

Fine, I reply, don't care about them, and if you like don't care about Native Americans or Amish or urban African Americans or anybody else alive, either. That's your right as citizens and as scholars. Care about your archeology; do a fine job by your archeology, stick to your archeology. But don't masquerade applied archeology—or applied history, or applied architectural history or landscape architecture—as "cultural resource management." Because people believe you, and culture as a whole suffers.

My purpose here is not just to berate you, or to flagellate myself for our collective errors. I come, instead, to make a point, explain a position, and offer a suggestion.

To reiterate the point, we need to be careful about what we are communicating. Through carelessness, we have communicated to planners and federal agencies that they need consider impacts only on archeological sites and old buildings in order to address NEPA's call for ensuring culturally pleasing surroundings, preserving cultural aspects of the national heritage, and supporting diversity. We have thus allowed other types of cultural resources to get sold down the river—which ought to trouble us as anthropologists. We have also, as a result, failed to create a CRM that is relevant to a wide range of cultural concerns. On the contrary, we have created a CRM that is relevant only to a narrow range of specialists. If we do not suffer in the political process as a result, it will be by sheer dumb luck.

This is why—and this is the position I want to explain—I support radical change in the legal underpinnings of CRM. Actually it's not the only reason, but it's an important one. I think we have created such an irresponsible, irrelevant, counterproductive system under the rubric of CRM that the best thing to do with it would be to tear it apart and start over again.

Sort of like a lot of public housing projects. Do away with the National Register, do away with the Advisory Council, do away with Section 106, and rebuild with the benefit of what we've learned over the last thirty years.

I hasten to add that I don't expect a clean demolition and rebuilding of the CRM laws to occur. Rather, I anticipate only a gradual deterioration in the level of rigor, honor, and intelligence with which Section 106 review, at least, is carried out. In point of fact, this deterioration is already well underway. This will not eliminate the need for CRM, however; it will only make it less and less wise to tie the practice of CRM closely to the interests of the National Register and of the Advisory Council.

This brings me to my recommendation, which is that the CRM community—by which I do *not* mean archeologists alone—should make a deliberate attempt to reinvent itself. In so doing, the community should develop a broader vision, and ally itself with a broader range of interests, under a broader range of legal authorities.

I've alluded a couple of times to Social Impact Assessment (SIA). SIA has a long and somewhat convoluted history as part of NEPA review and in other countries has been extremely important in assuring that community cultural values are considered in project planning. In this country, for various reasons that I'm only beginning to understand and don't have time to discuss here, SIA was substantially captured by the economists in the early 1980s, and sociocultural concerns have tended to receive short shrift in NEPA analyses since then. An "Interorganizational Committee on Social Impact Assessment" has recently taken important

11

steps to clarify what SIA is about.[9] After substantial study, the Committee has published *Guidelines and Principles for Social Impact Assessment*.[10] The *Guidelines and Principles* define the subject matter of SIA and outline recommended procedures for use by practitioners in addressing it—in defining project impacts on the sociocultural environment and helping resolve impacts that are adverse. The *Guidelines and Principles* are far too long even to outline here, but they're excellent and I recommend them for your consideration.

I think that CRM would be well advised to do something similar, and in fact to build upon the SIA Committee's work, consult with the SIA Committee to seek common ground, and see if there isn't a basis for building an approach to analyzing impacts on the sociocultural environment that combines CRM and SIA and includes all the stuff that today tends to fall through the cracks between them. I propose that the organizations concerned with CRM form a committee to pursue this possibility, in coordination with the members of the SIA Committee.

As an initial contribution to this effort I want to offer the following definition of the cultural environment that I believe should be the subject of combined CRM and SIA studies as part of any environmental impact analysis:

> The cultural environment comprises all those aspects of the physical environment that relate to human culture and society, together with the cultural institutions that hold communities together and link them to their surroundings. The cultural environment thus includes, but is not limited to:
> * the ways in which people live, work, play, relate to one another, organize to meet their needs, and generally cope as members of society in general and their communities in particular;
> * the norms, values, and beliefs that guide and rationalize a community's perception of itself; and
> * the expressions of human culture and history in the physical environment, including culturally significant landscapes, historic and archeological sites, buildings, structures, districts and objects, places that are regarded as sacred or powerful by practitioners of any religion, places needed for traditional subsistence activities and cultural practices, and artifacts and documents of cultural and historical significance.

This definition is shamelessly plagiarized from the work of the SIA Committee, but it blends in the traditional property-based concerns of CRM. I think it could serve as the basis for a combined, holistic approach to the analysis of impacts on, and to the management of, "cultural resources" in their entirety—as opposed to "cultural resources" as imagined two decades ago by a bunch of half-soused archeologists.

Notes

1. From NPS-28, the National Park Service's overall internal cultural resources management guidelines.
2. Schuldenrein 1995. I mean no offense to Joe Schuldenrein or to his paper, which I think is excellent, but his title was truly irresistible.
3. The conference was the 1974 Cultural Resource Management Conference at the Federal Center in Denver, whose *Proceedings* were published under the editorship of William D. Lipe and Alexander J. Lindsay Jr. as *Museum of Northern Arizona Technical Series No. 14*. It is my distinct recollection that the term *CRM* was first proposed in the bar at the airport where many conferees were hanging out and imbibing after all flights out were cancelled due to snow. In the introduction to the *Proceedings*, however, Lipe and Lindsay allude to two "CRM seminars" held in Tempe, Arizona, in 1973 (*Proceedings*, p. x). In support of my own recollection, in skimming the *Proceedings*, I find only two other references to "cultural resources"—both rather glancing—by L. E. Aten (p. 94) and James Judge (p. 186). I have seen the term nowhere in the pre-1974 literature. I conclude that the term was in some use among southwestern applied archeologists prior to 1974, but only began to gain broad currency with the 1974 conference and its somewhat sodden aftermath.
4. Specifically, Section 101(b), NEPA's statement of federal government responsibilities.
5. King and Rafuse 1994.
6. The reference (in the report) is to *How to Write Quality EISs and EAs*, Larry H. Freeman, Shipley Associates, Bountiful, Utah, 1992. *How to Write* is a widely used source on the conduct of NEPA analyses and the preparation of NEPA documents. On the page referenced, Freeman outlines variables that should be considered in analyzing impacts on the social environment.
7. Parker and King 1990.
8. *Time* 146:17, October 23, 1995. One of the cover stories under the heading "Don't Tread on Me: An Inside Look at the West's Growing Rebellion" deals with Nye County, its inhabitants' readiness to fight for their traditional lifeways,

and their equation of federal requirements for "archeological appraisals" with governmental oppression (pp. 62, 66).

9. The Committee includes representatives of the Rural Sociological Society, the American Psychological Association, the American Sociological Association, the American Anthropological Association and Society for Applied Anthropology, and the International Association for Impact Assessment, plus members at large.

10. Interorganizational Committee on Guidelines and Principles for Social Impact Assessment 1994.

2

It's Not Ethnography, Either

One of the themes I harp on in this book and elsewhere is the premise that CRM is not just a sort of applied archaeology. Nor, I insist, is it applied history, architectural history, historical architecture, landscape architecture, or any of the other academic disciplines that have traditionally spawned its practitioners. Another much belabored theme of mine is the idea that CRM is centrally about living people and their communities and the values they ascribe to aspects of the physical environment.

In view of the latter bias, you'd think I'd praise the editors of *CRM*, the National Park Service's magazine of happy news about historic preservation, for devoting the August 2001 issue[1] (Vol. 23, No. 5) to "People and Places." But no.

Actually there is much to praise in *CRM* 23:5, though like virtually every other issue it is so dominated by articles about National Park–related issues that its relevance to non-"Parkies" is questionable. But what spoils it, on the whole, is summed up by its subtitle: "The Ethnographic Connection."

The implication of this subtitle—that ethnography somehow encapsulates or represents CRM's interest in People and Places—infuses the whole issue, including even several of the papers that make interesting and useful points (e.g., Miki Crespi's thoughtful introductory paper, Larry Van Horn's interesting discussion of American Indian perspectives on the interpretation of the Manzanar internment camp, and Rachel Mason's and Janet Cohen's discussion of the federal subsistence program under the Alaska Native Claims Settlement Act). Almost every article, particularly if it was written by NPS personnel, beats the ethnography drum.

What's wrong with this? Well, just what is "ethnography," anyhow?

Crespi, having noted that ethnography is "a part of cultural anthropology; a social science addressing people in social contexts," cites a general textbook on the subject[2] to define it as a "bundle of methods and concepts."[3] This is the problem.

Ethnography—like archeology—is a body of method that's used in the enterprise of learning about human culture. It's all about getting and analyzing data for purposes of research. To characterize the people/place relationship as a matter of ethnography is to define it as a research topic rather than as a human value.

Try a couple of thought experiments. First, imagine a place that's important to you, the reader, as a person. Your church or synagogue or mosque, your family's favorite picnic spot, the place where you buried your pet turtle. Now imagine how you would describe how and why that place is important to you. Would you describe its value to you as "ethnographic"? I doubt it—unless perhaps you're an ethnographer. In fact, I'll bet that if someone else so described it you'd feel a bit insulted, like you (and perhaps others who share your values, maybe your whole community) were reduced to a scientific specimen of some kind.

Closer to the point, perhaps, imagine yourself trying to explain why money should be spent to preserve, say, the sweetgrass stands needed by African American basketmakers in coastal South Carolina. Or why a highway should be rerouted to avoid impacts on an Indian tribe's vision quest sites. Which is going to be more persuasive to the folks who make the funding and routing decisions: emphasizing the importance of the places involved as elements of the environment treasured by living communities, or as "ethnographic resources"? I suppose it's conceivable that in the rarified atmosphere of the National Park Service the latter characterization might be effective, but in the real world it won't carry much political weight.

The National Park Service ethnographers largely responsible for *CRM* 23:5 will doubtless protest that they use the term "ethnography" merely as a convenient handle for all those real-world values that living communities care about. No doubt; I don't question their good intentions, and in NPS what they say may work. NPS after all is the heir to the Bureau of American Ethnology and has a long and honorable tradition of paying attention to ethnographic matters. But outside the Park Service I'm quite sure that calling living communities and their values "ethnographic" is counterproductive. It's counterproductive in the communities themselves, which may not want to be regarded as objects of scientific inquiry, and it's counterproductive in the world of agency decision making, where social science tends to be seen as something of a frill but where real people still (sometimes) have some drag.

But it's also counterproductive in a larger way, I think, in that it makes us, the practitioners of CRM, put the wrong spin on our evaluation of things.

Leaving ethnography for a moment, consider archeology. Suppose we're dealing with an Indian tribe's ancestral village site. Consider the difference between calling it an "ancestral village site" and calling it an "archeological site." The latter term inevitably conjures up the image of something that can be dug up, whose value can be preserved in the form of a research report and artifacts on a shelf, that's important because of what it can teach us—outsiders to the community—about the past. The former implies something quite different—a place where the ancestors of a living community lived. I suggest that when we think about ancestral village sites first and foremost as archeological sites, we elevate their research value to nonparticipants in the descendant community over their sociocultural, emotional, and spiritual importance to the community. I think that's a problem if we're going to have a cultural resources management that reflects and respects the cultural values of living people.

The same principle applies to using "ethnographic" to refer to living cultures and their values. The subject of ethnography is by definition the subject of research, and while ethnographers may prefer that their subjects stay alive and persist, their basic professional charge is to document and learn from them. There's nothing wrong with that, just as there's nothing wrong with archeological research. But the ethnographic value of a community no more reflects its cultural importance to its members than the archeological value of a cemetery reflects its importance to the descendants of those buried there.

Ethnography, like archeology, is a tool. It's a very useful tool, and one that probably ought to be applied a lot more widely than it is in the practice

17

of CRM. But it's not what CRM, with respect to living communities, is about. And ironically, I'll wager that use of the term actually discourages the widespread use of ethnography in CRM. After all, why should an agency personnel officer or budget analyst pay for ethnography for its own sake or hire ethnographers to do ethnography? Agencies budget and hire to meet their mission needs, comply with legal requirements, and respond to what the agencies understand to be the public interest. The concerns of communities about impacts on their ways of life and their treasured places are important enough to drive budget and personnel decisions. Only in NPS, perhaps, with its history of ethnographic involvement and its public interpretive mission, is ethnography, *qua* ethnography, enough to influence such decisions.

Notes

1. NPS 2001.
2. Ellen 1984.
3. Crespi 2001.

3

An Uninspired Centerpiece: The National Register of Historic Places

The National Register of Historic Places is the U.S. version of an institution that's fundamental to the historic preservation systems of all European countries and at least most ex-colonies. Variously called a Register, a Schedule, a List, it's supposed to be a roster of all those places deemed to be historically important by some governmental authority. In the United States, the authority is the National Park Service, represented by the Keeper of the National Register. The Keeper heads a small staff that quite literally keeps the Register—keeps it up, maintains it, oversees its expansion, promotes it, determines what's eligible for inclusion in it.

The Register widely advertises itself, and is generally uncritically taken to be, the "centerpiece" of the national historic preservation program. It's safe to assume that the same perception attaches to other national schedules, registers, and similar lists. It's understandable; surely it makes sense for the national program—any national program—to focus on the protection of places that have been determined by some cognizant authority like the Keeper to be worthy of preservation and accordingly added to a list of such places.

But when you think about it, it's hard to escape the conclusion that a centrally defined and maintained register is a rather undemocratic (and for that matter unrepublican, antifederalist) institution. Who in the world is the Keeper, however august and expert she may be, to tell the people of

South Roughrock, Montana, which of their buildings and sites are "really" significant?

As a physical list of places in the United States, the Register has its origins in two earlier lists maintained by the Park Service—the list of National Historic Landmarks designated under the Historic Sites Act of 1935 and the list of buildings and structures documented from the 1930s onward by the Historic American Buildings Survey. But as a concept, the Register has its roots in the historic preservation programs of the European nations. This is not to say that the European colonial powers imposed the idea on us. England did not establish a Royal Schedule of Historic Properties in its North American colonies, France didn't create *le Registre Colonial des Endroits Historiques,* and Spain didn't set forth a list of places that made up *el Patrimonio Colonial.* But all the European countries had developed lists as the centerpieces of their historic preservation programs by World War II. In the wake of the war, the reconstruction of many ravaged European cities included the restoration—sometimes from the ground up—of bombed-out scheduled buildings and districts. In 1964 to 1965, when the U.S. Conference of Mayors in the United States sponsored a White House conference and European study tour that would lead to the seminal volume *With Heritage So Rich,*[1] and thence to the National Historic Preservation Act, the models studied by the conferees were those provided by the Europeans. And the conferees viewed with alarm the fact that the United States had no master list. Accordingly, one of the main things the NHPA did was to authorize and direct NPS to "expand and maintain" a National Register.

So since the mid-1960s we've had our Register, just like other developed countries. Like other countries, we've grown to take it for granted, if not necessarily to love it. But should we? Is it necessary? Is it sufficient? Does it really contribute to, or detract from, an intelligent national program of historic preservation? Are there better alternatives?

In the European nations from whose preservation systems the Register was derived, objects of antiquity ("archeological resources" in the United States) are typically regarded as the property of the state. Historic buildings, sites, and monuments have always been a bit trickier to deal with, because they often quite certainly are *not* the property of the state. Many belong to religious orders, local governments, and private entities, and many continue in active use. The desire to preserve some such properties led to the practice of governmental "listing," "scheduling," or "registering" places that were seen to have sufficient importance to warrant possible government acquisition or the imposition of government controls over the actions of their owners.

Listing, of course, had to be performed by someone, so governments began to develop ministries of culture, bureaus of archaeology and architecture, and similar institutions, with listing among their major responsibilities. Listing had financial implications both for government and for the owners of historic properties, so professional procedures, criteria, and standards were developed for balancing historical value against conflicting economic, social, and political interests. The general premise underlying the registration process was that if a place was sufficiently historic to be registered, it ought to be preserved in place despite conflicting claims to the economic use of the land it occupied. Conversely, if conflicting claims were sufficiently important (or were backed by sufficient political muscle) to require the historic property to be sacrificed, it should not be listed.

So the Register has its roots in a system that lists places that government deems sufficiently worthy of preservation, and of sufficiently little worth for any other sort of use, to merit government acquisition, protection in place, and sometimes restoration. All the European systems have evolved in various ways, but the idea of a list of historic properties in which government should invest remains basic to all. As does the idea of an authoritative governmental body, made up of preservation professionals, to decide what should be listed and to maintain the list as it grows.

There are a couple of problems with this model when it's applied to the modern United States. First, of course, is our sturdy tradition of private ownership, our resolute desire to keep government—particularly the federal government—at arm's length. The idea that the Feds can designate a place as historic and hence govern how it will be used—even with compensation for the erstwhile owner—is repugnant to our national traditions. The second problem is that with respect to listed properties, it gives preservation priority over all other uses—not really very realistic in a dynamic modern state with a wide range of social and political responsibilities and a bustling capitalist economy.

The founders of the U.S. historic preservation program recognized these problems and sought to address them both in Section 106. In the language of Section 106, the federal government does not take it upon itself necessarily to *preserve* historic properties, either by acquiring them or by limiting their modification; it merely requires itself to "take into account" the effects of its actions on such properties. No restrictions whatever are placed on nonfederal parties, except where they are involved with the federal government through programs of assistance or licenses.

A creative and thoughtful solution, but it left the Register with an identity crisis that has persisted into the present. Is the Register a list of the nation's best and brightest properties, in whose permanent protection government should invest, or is it simply a list of places that ought to be considered in planning? A list that approximates the European models that are the Register's ancestors would inevitably be small and highly selective; a list of places that are just to be "considered" can and should be much broader. But how can one embrace both identities within a single system of evaluation?

There is another problem with the European model, which I've alluded to above. It's fundamentally centrist, elitist, antidemocratic. After all, the whole notion grew up in the context of kings, princes, and a very powerful central government. Transplanting this sort of thing to a republican democracy is tricky business.

The founders tried to address this problem, too, by explicitly specifying that the Register would embrace properties not only of "national" significance but also of "state" and "local" significance. An important concept, but not really very logical. What business is it of the federal government to decide what's important to a state or to a locality? To say nothing of entities like Indian tribes, which were not on the founders' radar screens.

Despite these internal contradictions, the Register has grown and become firmly established at the core of the national historic preservation program. In the 1980s, however, some of the fault lines in the Register's intellectual bedrock began to move. The Register began to be accused of being too inclusive, letting too much get listed. Were the Register understood simply as a list of places to be considered in planning, this accusation would make very little sense and would be relatively easy to rebut. But the Register is both a list of places to be considered *and* a list of places in which government should invest money and over which it should assert control. This made charges of overinclusiveness harder to dismiss.

The Register responded to this challenge by insisting on ever-higher levels of "professionalism" in nominations and—to the extent it controlled them—determinations of eligibility. Technical standards for paperwork became tighter and tighter, and it became more and more important to show that the paperwork had been completed by a properly qualified professional—typically an architectural historian, historian, or archeologist. One effect of this was to drive the cost of nominations ever higher, farther and farther out of the reach of plain citizens, to say nothing of minority communities and low-income groups. Another was to make the Register less and less relevant to local concerns and vice versa. The Register became more and more a list of places officially determined to be important to preservation professionals, by preservation professionals, for preservation professionals.

The publication of National Register *Bulletin* 38 in 1990[2] was an attempt at something of a course correction. *Bulletin* 38 asserted that "traditional cultural properties"—places important to communities in maintaining their ongoing cultural identity—could be eligible for the Register and discussed how to identify and document them. It's a rather sad commentary on the Olympian heights to which the Register had drifted that *Bulletin* 38 even had to be written; it's even sadder that its implementation has caused so much angst. Questions immediately arose, and continue to arise, about what kinds of professional qualifications one needed to evaluate a "TCP" and how one was to collect the data thought necessary to fill out the Register's forms.

The basic problem lies in the Register's unresolved identity crisis: Is it a list of elite properties that the dominant society wants to preserve, or is it a very broad list of places that should be considered in planning? The Register staff can't resolve this problem, though its practice tends to favor the elite identity while its rhetoric embraces the populist.

In my training and consulting practice, I have come to advise students and clients to keep as far away from the National Register as they possibly can. Do not nominate anything unless you have a really good, practical reason. Avoid formal eligibility determinations by the Keeper if there's any way to do so. Work things out locally, where there's flexibility and you're not likely to get questions and answers that make sense only to an architectural historian steeped in the mystique of the nomination form. Recognize that under the Section 106 regulations there's no requirement for any particular level of documentation in order to consider a property eligible; the consulting parties, if they agree, can just do it, and in most cases it's better all around to make the assumption and get on with figuring out how to manage the place.

For my money, the National Register is not the centerpiece of the national program. It's not so much the program's heart as its appendix—of questionable value but hanging there ready to cause trouble. If anything is really at the core of the national program it's Section 106 review, and the best way to do Section 106 review is with as little involvement of the National Register as possible.

But as long as the Register exists, with its identity conflict unresolved, it will continue to trouble us, permitting locally important properties to be destroyed because they aren't recognized as important by professionals, or don't fit into boxes on a form; costing unnecessary time and money; confusing the public and its representatives about the purpose and priorities of the national program; and discriminating against the cultural concerns of minority and low-income citizens.

There is, perhaps, some need for a list of historic properties in which the federal government should invest its limited resources. A small, selective National Register might serve this purpose, though I think there are better ways to meet this need. The tax credits that can be applied for when one properly rehabilitates a National Register property are certainly a good thing, but it's not hard to imagine having such credits without having a National Register—let locally maintained lists suffice. As for the Register's alleged planning functions, I think we'd do far better with a Section 106 process uncoupled from the Register. Such a process could be designed to ascertain, in any given case, whether there were historic preservation (or broader cultural resource) conflicts to be resolved and then seek to resolve them through broad-based stakeholder consultation.

But how would we know if there were conflicts, if we didn't have the Register and its criteria to use in measuring the significance of properties with which conflicts might occur? Well, for years and years before there was a National Register, we in archeology were able to figure out where there were conflicts between modern land use and important archeological sites and what to do about them. I feel sure that architectural historians and other professionals could do just as well with the kinds of properties they're concerned about, and as for places important to communities—well, here we are again: Ask the people. I think we could have quite a happy federal historic preservation planning process without a Register. I think such a process could effect better historic preservation than the present one does, and that it could waste a lot less time and money on pointless arguments—most of which are relevant only to people for whom maintaining lists is an end in itself.

Notes

1. U.S. Conference of Mayors 1967.
2. Parker and King 1990.

4

*The Hester**

Hester Davis[1] has been unwavering in her vision of archeology as a public enterprise. She was also among the several parents of "cultural resource management" as that term is usually if unfortunately understood—the practice of archeology and sometimes other culture-related disciplines under the historic preservation and environmental laws.

I think it's safe to say that Hester has always seen CRM as consistent with her vision of a public archeology. After all, CRM is aimed at making sure that the public's interest in archeological sites (and occasionally other kinds of cultural resources) is honored in the treatment of such resources. And there is no reason why the public should not be actively involved in the CRM enterprise.

However, CRM has not developed in an entirely public-oriented way.

CRM has had a sort of centripetal tendency to devolve into doing what is necessary to please the State Historic Preservation Officer (SHPO)—to achieve "clearance" for one's project. If the SHPO is responsive to the public, fine, but if not, whatever public interests may exist in the archeology or the project's effects on it are likely to be ignored.

---

*Originally titled "Public Archeology and CRM: For Whom and Why?" presented in the symposium entitled "Hester's Legacy in Practice," Society for American Archaeology Annual Meeting, March 27, 1999.

At the same time, more and more emphasis has been given to "professionalism" in the conduct of CRM. This does not necessarily mean behaving in a professional manner (whatever that is). Rather, it's taken to mean having the appropriate degrees, years in practice, and other credentials.

As a result, what purports to be a CRM project—say, a data recovery project or the writing of an installation "cultural resource management plan" often devolves into simply a bunch of Ph.D.s and MAs doing what they think the SHPO has told them to do. The public may not even know about the project. Public involvement, if it happens at all, may amount to a post-project brochure or display. Perhaps there will be a guided tour of the dig every now and then, perhaps an article in the local newspaper. Or maybe none of these things. And what the public wants done with the archeological resource is seldom even assessed, let alone reflected in the work.

Naturally there are distinguished exceptions to this rule, and there are also projects that for various reasons can't or shouldn't be open to public input and participation. And what's happened to CRM is nobody's fault, really; it's just something that's evolved. But the fact remains that really effective public participation in CRM, and public influence over the content and character of CRM-based work, is very limited. And that, I think, is unfortunate.

Is there anything we can do to improve the situation? I have a few suggestions.

First, we need to be careful not to make the situation worse. The National Park Service has a tremendous opportunity to make things worse if and when it once again embarks on an effort to respond to Section 112 of the National Historic Preservation Act by developing and revising professional standards. In carrying out its duties under this section, NPS should try to be careful not to do anything to shut out the interested public from full participation in archeology and other aspects of CRM.

Second, those in the professional community who insist on opposing the use of "paraprofessionals" and volunteers should grow up, get real, and try to help the agencies that need such help develop and maintain it in a responsible manner.[2]

Third, everyone who's involved in writing or rewriting standards, guidelines, and the like for identification of archeological sites and other historic properties should make sure they include an explicit section on

27

eliciting and documenting public interests in whatever it is that's being identified—with the caveat, of course, that confidentiality needs to be protected where it's relevant. After all, we do background research to ascertain, among other things, what professional interests there are in an area's archeological resources—what research has been done in the past, what research interests may make an archeological site eligible for the National Register. Why not give equal consideration to the interests of plain folks—be they local historical societies, archeological groups, artifact collectors, minority groups, property owners, schools, or whoever?

Finally, if nothing else I suggest that every SHPO office, every CRM contracting firm, every federal agency that does substantial CRM and every sizeable CRM project have a staff member formally designated as "The Hester." The Hester should have the job of keeping public interests foremost in her or his mind and of bugging everyone else to make sure that those interests are considered in planning and implementing projects. In most cases The Hester would not be a full-time assignment; it would be an ancillary duty. But it should be an official, formally designated duty, embodied in position descriptions and contracts using words something like the following:

> The Hester serves as the public's interface with the project, program, or office and reminds other members of the staff of the need to be responsive to public interests and concerns. The Hester actively seeks to identify such interests and concerns and to find ways to satisfy the former and resolve the latter. The Hester is responsible for ascertaining what public interests in the project/program/office exist and for working with staff to address such interests, where possible through cooperative efforts with outside organizations and individuals.

Recognizing a formal staff function like this would go far, I think, toward preventing professionals and administrators from forgetting the public whose interests we're all supposed to be serving. And giving the function the name I propose, letting it sink into the jargon until it is used unconsciously—until it is perhaps given the verb form "to Hester" or an adjectival form as in "That was a really Hester project"—would be a suitable way to honor the woman who arguably is the mother of American CRM and who has always had the public's interests at heart.

Notes

1. Hester Davis has been for some decades Arkansas's state archaeologist and a major force in the development of CRM in the United States, who retired shortly before the paper this chapter is based on was presented.

2. Such programs, using agency personnel and others without professional archeological (or other CRM) credentials to do CRM work after training, and with professional supervision, are carried out by elements of the Forest Service, Bureau of Land Management, and Natural Resource Conservation Service, among others. Many professionals express shock and horror at such programs.

5

Process vs. Preservation: A False Dichotomy

Participants in the classes I teach for the National Preservation Institute (NPI) are asked at the end of each session to fill out a course evaluation. Skimming the evaluations after a recent class (something I always do reluctantly and with trepidation), I ran into a rather snippy comment that "It is unclear whether the instructor believes in preservation or merely in process."

The comment made me think, not only about what I believe in, but also generally about the oft-expressed dichotomy between preservation (often under the code word "substance") and process in Section 106 review. Advocates like the National Trust for Historic Preservation regularly bemoan the preoccupation of the Advisory Council on Historic Preservation (ACHP) with "process"—"The Council doesn't care about the outcome, as long as all the 'i's' are dotted and the 't's' are crossed." The ACHP's putative leadership tends to be stung by such criticism and to vow more attention to the substantive outcome of the Section 106 process—meaning, apparently, that the process should result in more preservation of historic places than it does. They don't succeed; it would be political suicide if they did, and whatever else the ACHP may be interested in, it is not interested in its own demise. But they feel bad about their failure, like they ought to be better preservationists, more like the National Trust or maybe NPS. The result is an ACHP that is unsure of its purpose in life and that devotes less intellectual attention to the Section 106 process than to the formulation of widely ignored policy recommendations favoring better preservation.

I don't think the ACHP has any reason to be ashamed of emphasizing process; I think it would do well to stake out a position as the rigorous proponent of good process, irrespective of outcome. But the preservation versus process nondebate (because *nobody* ever seems to argue that process should be paramount) has dimensions that go beyond the ACHP. Cultural resource managers in general are expected—by clients, by the public, by themselves—to be proponents for "the resource," and when (as is very often the case) they cannot achieve what they think to be good preservation of the resource, they feel bad about it. I don't think they should, and I don't think I should. So to answer my classroom critic, I believe in process.

This is not to say that I don't think that historic properties ought to be preserved. Far from it—I very much favor keeping historic properties with us and making good use of them. I think it's among my jobs to promote such preservation through my participation in Section 106 review and other CRM processes. But I think the rational way to do this is by promoting good process, not by promoting preservation *uber alles*.

Whatever armchair historic preservationists may think, we are seldom confronted in CRM with absolute conflicts between preservation of great old things and their unmitigated destruction by evildoers who don't appreciate their value. Most often we deal with conflicts over properties that some people think are pretty important while others do not, whose preservation conflicts with projects that some people at least honestly think are necessary and in the public interest, and whose loss can to some extent at least be mitigated. Are we good preservationists only if we insist on the preservation of every historic property, regardless of its significance, its long-term potential for survival, the level of public interest in it, and the justifications for destroying or altering it? I'm sure that even my classroom critic would say "No, that would be ridiculous."

But if that's ridiculous, then what preservation advocacy is *not* ridiculous? Well, I imagine my critic saying, advocating the preservation of really important places isn't ridiculous. Okay, I reply, so how do we decide what's really important?

My critic might point to the National Register criteria (36 CFR 60.4) as the bases for deciding. But the Register criteria are very broad and inclusive. If we preserved everything that now is usually considered eligible for the Register, it would be tantamount to preserving everything that anybody can more or less demonstrate has some historical, architectural, archeological, or cultural significance. The Register criteria get us nowhere, unless they're reinterpreted much more narrowly than they now are or totally revamped to describe only the crème de la crème of historic properties. And even if we were able to so rethink the criteria, what would we do with them? How would we apply them to specific properties? How would we decide whether they were met?

And while we think about that, what about the importance of the projects that may cause damage to such properties? Suppose that tomorrow we experience an outbreak of a new virus that threatens to wipe out all life on earth, and the only source of the super-rare mineral that can be used to produce an antidote is the soil directly under Mount Vernon. Do we preserve the homeplace of our country's father for aliens to appreciate when they visit our lifeless world some ages hence? Probably not. But if we can sacrifice Mount Vernon to save life on earth, then can we sacrifice, say, the Statue of Liberty to save all human life? The Golden Gate Bridge to save everyone in San Francisco? And how do we decide?

Or what if what was proposed at Mount Vernon was not its destruction but the construction of a well-disguised interpretive center underneath it, simultaneously reinforcing the foundations against seismic stress? Would this be okay, or would it not? How would we decide?

The point is that there are lots of historic places, with lots of different kinds of significance, and lots of different kinds of projects, with lots of different kinds of justifications, and lots of different kinds of effects, and you can't contend with this kind of variability simply by promoting some abstract vision of perfect preservation. You need *processes* for deciding what's important, how justified actions are that may affect important things, what alternatives are available to achieve a proposed action's purposes, and what to do about the effects of justified alternatives. We can argue about whether our current processes, notably the Section 106 process, are all they should be, but suggesting that attention to process is somehow antithetical to preservation is not useful in resolving such arguments. It leads us to see process as something dirty, unimportant, beneath us, so we don't think about it, or try to improve it, and we remain stuck with processes that don't work very well.

I said earlier that no one defends process. That's true in preservation land, but of course it's not in other contexts. Mediators and other practitioners of alternative (to litigation) dispute resolution (ADR) routinely promote process, and within certain basic (though much debated) ethical bounds a mediator is supposed to be neutral about substance. I think that a specialist in resolving conflicts between the past and the future—and what else is a cultural resource manager?—must adopt a similar stance. We should be concerned about "the resource," just as, say, a divorce mediator should be concerned about the interests of a soon-to-be ex-wife. But just as the divorce mediator must be equally sensitive to the needs of the soon-to-be ex-husband, a cultural resource manager needs to appreciate the interests of change agents. CRM, at least as it applies to the management of modern society's impacts on cultural resources, is all about seeking balance between equally justified, if often conflicting, interests.

This is why people trained exclusively in a given "preservation discipline" like architectural history or archeology don't necessarily make very good cultural resource managers and why even training people in multiple disciplines doesn't necessarily help much. A few years ago I sat in a meeting of the National Council for Preservation Education (NCPE), and watched its members flagellate themselves for failing to imbue their students with a proper "preservation ethic." Which meant, apparently, that they should never, never, never go along with the demolition of a historic building, or at least never do so without feeling terribly bad about it. I can think of few attitudes that are more antithetical to responsible cultural resource management or more conducive to premature and unnecessary ulcers. Or more indicative of why the training of cultural resource managers should not be guided by architectural historians and archeologists. Effective cultural resource management, I believe, requires the ability to find creative and balanced solutions to conflicts, through process management, a lot more than it requires skill in recognizing building types or drawing stratigraphic profiles.

Part II

Thinking about Impact Assessment and Mitigation

In the United States, most people who call themselves "cultural resource managers" work most of the time in impact assessment and mitigation—figuring out what damage federal agency decisions will cause to "cultural resources" and doing things (sometimes) to reduce the damage. That's not what the term suggests, of course, and there are CRM people who actually manage resources, but impact assessment and mitigation are the areas where most of the money is, so it's what most of us do. Some CRM people bemoan this fact and pontificate about getting "beyond impact assessment."[1] I think they're naïve. Like it or not, the world has lots of things to do besides CRM—things like food production, economic development, environmental protection, and defense. Most of our efforts are always and properly going to be directed toward harmonizing the projects required for such purposes with the perpetuation of culturally valued resources.

At the core of impact assessment practice in CRM are two legal requirements—Section 102(2)(C) of the National Environmental Policy Act (NEPA) and Section 106 of the National Historic Preservation Act (NHPA). The first requires federal agencies to analyze, document, and consider the effects of their actions (including those they assist or permit) on all aspects of the environment, including its cultural aspects. The second specifically calls upon them to consider the impacts of such actions on "historic properties"—physical places included in or eligible for a

"National Register of Historic Places" maintained by the National Park Service (NPS). NEPA review is done under regulations[2] issued by the Council on Environmental Quality (CEQ). Section 106 review follows regulations[3] issued by the Advisory Council on Historic Preservation (ACHP). Other environmental and cultural resource requirements like the American Indian Religious Freedom Act and Executive Order 12898 (Environmental Justice) influence cultural resource practice under NEPA and Section 106.[4]

Section 106 is by far the more familiar of the two legal authorities to most cultural resource managers and is the major focus of the several chapters that follow. There's a lot about practice under Section 106 that bothers me—that I think makes for inept, inadequate, inefficient review that fails to meet the law's intent. Some problems reflect inartful regulatory draftsmanship by the ACHP. Others result from bizarre interpretations of laws and regulations by the federal agencies that are supposed to implement them. Still others are the products of practice itself—the strategies, systems, assumptions, biases, and myths developed by agency staff, State and Tribal Historic Preservation Officers (SHPOs, THPOs), consultants, and professional organizations who try to interpret and apply Section 106 and related legal requirements.

The eight chapters that follow deal with a few of the major problems I see in Section 106 practice. The first contends with the fact that most people who do what they think is Section 106 review are actually doing something else. The second questions whether the Section 106 review system is worth maintaining at all, and suggests alternatives. The third discusses the effects of sloppy terminology in Section 106 review, and the fourth addresses the way Section 106 does or does not handle a particular kind of project effect—impact on the quality of the visual environment. The fifth provides an example of the complexities that may arise from the interplay between Section 106 and other laws, and the sixth suggests that the actual requirements of the law may provide ways to resolve seemingly intractable problems in Section 106 compliance. The seventh chapter is about State Historic Preservation Officers and the direction they give agencies, and the last chapter is about consultants—the people who do the bulk of the day-to-day grunt work of impact assessment. It asks a question that I think is very important, but that is getting answered through inattention today—is it a consultant's responsibility to provide objective advice or to advance a client's purposes?

Notes

1. Usually expressed as "Beyond 106" with reference to the assessment requirement with which CRM practitioners are usually most familiar.

2. 40 CFR 1500–1508.

3. 36 CFR 800.

4. See King 1998a for an overview of CRM laws and practice and King 2000 for detailed treatment of Section 106 review.

What Is Section 106 Review Anyhow? Two Views

E verybody in CRM thinks they know what Section 106 review is. What's understood to be the process, however, varies widely from person to person—despite the existence of regulations that certainly describe it in detail, if not with crystalline clarity.

The basic Section 106 process is described in the Advisory Council's regulations at 36 CFR 800.3–7. The requirement of law from which the regulations spring—Section 106 of the National Historic Preservation Act itself—tells federal agencies to "take into account" the effects of their actions on historic properties. The regulations say that to do this, an agency must consult with the State Historic Preservation Officer or Tribal Historic Preservation Officer (SHPO, THPO) and other concerned parties, identify historic properties, determine what effect (if any) the agency's action may have on them, and try to reach agreement on how to resolve effects that are adverse. That, of course, is only the most skeletal of outlines; there are lots of specific procedures by which each of the above requirements is to be met.

It's long been my impression—from talking with CRM practitioners, reading reports, discussing the matter with people in my classes, interacting with others on the Internet—that there's another whole shadow universe of "Section 106" practice out there—something that people understand to be Section 106 review even though its relationship to the process set forth in the regulations is tenuous. It was hard to objectify this impression until one day recently when I stumbled on the World Wide Web site of a large CRM firm that in the interests of protecting the innocent will remain nameless (hereinafter, "the firm"). One of the services provided to visitors of this site is a "Guide to Compliance."[1] Early on, the "Guide" makes it clear that what it purports to present is the Section 106 process.

It would far exceed any reasonable page limit for this chapter to rigorously compare the "Guide" with the regulations, and it would bore my readers silly. Let's look at some key points of contrast, however, and see what we can make of them. I'll paraphrase the regulations, since they're quite long and complicated and readily available online and in hard copy from the Advisory Council (and discussed in King 2000). I'll largely paraphrase what the "Guide" has to say, too, in order to avoid any appearance of copyright infringement or of harassing the firm.

Initiating Review

How an agency—or a nonfederal applicant for a federal agency's assistance or permit—initiates Section 106 review is critical to the success of the review; it sets the stage for everything that follows. Among the major problems that beset Section 106 review is failure to initiate review at all. Another is delaying initiation until it's too late to do much about a project's impacts. So what the regulations and the "Guide" say about getting the process underway is very important.

What the Regulations Say

Section 800.3(a) of the regulations requires the agency to determine whether its action is an undertaking that requires review. If it is, then the agency is to coordinate review with its compliance with other laws, such as NEPA and NAGPRA, figure out which SHPO and/or THPO it needs to consult with, work out how it's going to involve the public, identify parties other than the SHPO/THPO with whom it needs to consult, and invite them to participate. All this is supposed to happen as early as possible in project planning, before significant money or time has been spent on the project.

What the "Guide" Says

The "Guide" tells us that the first step is for the "lead agency" to notify the SHPO. It also suggests that the lead agency at this point must determine whether the project is likely to have an adverse effect on "archaeological or historical sites." The lead agency then advises whoever is responsible for the project that "these cultural resources must be considered." It may at this point require that a survey be done or accede to the SHPO's insistence on one. If so, the "Guide" says, this usually leads to a three-phase "consideration" process.

The firm appears to be speaking to nonfederal parties required to participate in Section 106 review by federal agencies, so naturally the things it emphasizes are different from what the regulations emphasize. Still, it's interesting that its focus of attention is entirely on the SHPO, that there's no discussion of involving others (even THPOs), or of planning public participation. Nothing that says the work needs to get underway early in project planning, either.

Identification

Having gotten review underway, the agency sets out to identify historic properties that may be affected.

What the Regulations Say

At Section 800.4, the regulations first tell agencies to undertake "scoping." That is, they are to figure out what they need to do to identify historic properties. They do this in consultation with the SHPO and THPO. They first identify the "area of potential effects," or APE—the area or areas within which the action may have effects of any kind on historic properties. They review background data on the area and seek information from consulting parties and others, notably Indian tribes and Native Hawaiian groups (in Hawaii). Based on all this, they figure out what they need to do to make a "reasonable and good faith effort" to identify historic properties and then go forth and do it. Exactly what to do is left up to the scoping process. This is as it must be—there are far too many kinds of historic properties, that can be affected in far too many kinds of ways, to make it reasonable to prescribe a particular identification requirement.

What the "Guide" Says

The "Guide" is pretty expansive on the subject of identification, but blurs the distinction between identification and mitigation of impacts. It says that three phases of work are "usually" involved—an intensive survey "normally" called "Phase I," an assessment of specific properties known as Phase II, and a program of mitigation known as Phase III. It notes that in some regions a pre-intensive survey reconnaissance is called Phase I, or Phase Ia, with the intensive survey called Phase Ib or II, and that there are other permutations on the Phase theme. It then goes into considerable detail about "Phase I," the "cultural resource survey." This survey, it says, is about identifying archeological sites and historic structures (with a passing reference to traditional cultural properties); it advises that most states "require" that archeological identification be done by an archeologist and historic building identification be done by an architectural historian. It says the survey includes background research, defined as looking at data on previously recorded "sites" as well as general background research and discussions with "experts and inhabitants." Then one sometimes does a reconnaissance, but this is "usually not sufficient to satisfy federal regulations," which " require that all significant sites and structures . . . be identified." Apparently, one identifies all such properties by conducting an intensive field inspection.

This, of course, doesn't even approximate what the regulations say. In some cases it's directly inconsistent with them. The regulations, for example, nowhere say that a reconnaissance is seldom or never adequate, and they nowhere "require that all significant sites and structures be identified." They require a "reasonable and good faith effort," based on scoping—words that never appear in the "Guide." As part of scoping, they require the agency to identify the APE—a critically important step that the "Guide" doesn't deal with at all. There's a lot more that's wrong with what the "Guide" says about identification, I think, but it's not my purpose to beat up on the firm here; my purpose is to wonder how it is that a major consulting firm could have a view of the process that's so different from the way the Advisory Council describes it.

Let's skip ahead a bit.

Evaluation

What the Regulations Say

In essence, the regulations at 36 CFR 800.4(c) say that the agency is to evaluate possible historic properties it finds by applying the National Register Criteria (36 CFR 60.4) in consultation with the SHPO or

THPO. If the agency finds that the property is eligible, and the SHPO/THPO concurs, it's eligible. Ditto for ineligibility. If they don't agree, or if the Advisory Council or Keeper of the National Register so request (an important fail-safe mechanism to guard against the cutting of deals and the rolling of SHPOs), the agency takes the matter to the Keeper for a formal determination of eligibility. The regulations prescribe no standard for the documentation an agency and SHPO/THPO must have as the basis for agreeing on eligibility; it's whatever works under the circumstances.

What the "Guide" Says

Evaluation or "assessment," says the "Guide," is referred to as "Phase II." It generally involves digging shovel tests in archeological sites and detailed mapping, leading to analysis of results that forms the basis for deciding whether such sites are significant. Historic structures are evaluated based on an architectural historian's collection of detailed information about them, including background data, maps, and plans. All this leads to a report, which advises the client about "site" significance and provides treatment recommendations. The recipient submits this report to the lead agency for approval, which the lead agency grants or does not grant after consulting the SHPO. If the agency decides that a property is eligible for the Register, the project proponent "will need to mitigate any adverse impacts to the site."

Once again, there's very little resemblance between what the regulations say and what the "Guide" describes. As elsewhere, this may well reflect the fact that the Advisory Council is writing for agencies while the firm is writing for clients. That in itself is, I think, a useful observation, as we'll see. But the discrepancies go beyond those attributable to the use of language appropriate to different audiences. Where the regulations assume application to all kinds of historic properties, and emphasize application of the National Register Criteria, the "Guide" is overwhelmingly focused on archeological sites and mentions the National Register only in passing. Where the regulations specify no standard for documenting eligibility, the "Guide" goes into great detail about the fieldwork necessary to document significance. A critic might suggest that the firm is trying to get clients to believe that the kind of work that is its bread and butter is required by law, but I don't think that's it; I think that the firm and many,

many other CRM consultants actually believe that the regulations require what the "Guide" says.

The regulations go on to require that an agency, having found something eligible, follow some pretty specific procedures—including opportunities for more participation by consulting parties—to determine what effects it will have on the eligible property. Effects can be of all kinds—visual, atmospheric, audible; direct and indirect; cumulative. The "Guide" is silent on this element of the process—one would never know it exists. In the "Guide," the "assessment" phase flows directly into "mitigation." Let's follow.

Mitigation, or Resolution of Adverse Effects

Although under NEPA "mitigation" can mean a wide variety of things (including eliminating an adverse effect altogether; see 40 CFR 1508.20), the Advisory Council prefers a broader concept still and refers to "resolution of adverse effect." Mitigation (whatever it's taken to mean) is one way such effects may be resolved.

What the Regulations Say

At 36 CFR 800.6, agencies are directed to continue consultation both with those they're already consulting and with others who may have popped up during the preceding steps. More opportunities are to be provided for public participation. Consultation proceeds to one of two outcomes—either execution of a Memorandum of Agreement (MOA) specifying what will be done to resolve the adverse effects or a final Advisory Council comment following a failure to reach agreement. Detailed direction is provided about parties who must be consulted (SHPO/THPO, Indian tribes and Native Hawaiian groups, others who play roles in implementing the MOA, etc.), about documentation that must be provided to the consulting parties, about ways to pursue agreement with and without the Council's participation, and about what to do if consultation fails.

What the "Guide" Says

After assessment, the "Guide" tells us, one moves on to "Phase III," defined as "mitigation of adverse effects." Mitigation, we are told, may involve "avoiding the site," which is the least expensive thing to do but must be sold to the lead agency and SHPO. If one can't "avoid," one must do "data recovery." Data recovery in the case of structures involves HABS/HAER documentation;[2] in the case of archeological sites it means "digging large areas."

Consistent with its previously demonstrated tendencies, the "Guide" again conveys no notion that there's a process of consultation leading to "mitigation" decisions, or that there's any role for anyone other than the SHPO, "lead agency," and project proponent in making such decisions. And "mitigation" appears to mean one of two things—physical "avoidance" of a property or data recovery, either through archeological excavation or through architectural documentation. The firm seems unaware of such possibilities as building rehabilitation and reuse, archeological site burial, public interpretation of sites and structures, compensating for property loss by investment in other preservation activities, imposing design or development controls, and a host of other traditional and creative approaches to mitigation. And here as elsewhere, it doesn't seem to have tumbled to the fact that a historic property might be anything other than an archeological site or a historic structure.

Why the Discrepancies?

One could go on and on with this comparison, but—enough said. Clearly the "Guide" does not describe the Section 106 process as it's laid out in the regulations. Yet I feel pretty sure that—allowing for variation among states and regions—the firm's portrayal of the Section 106 process is closer to what most CRM consultants think the process is than is what's described in the regulations. At the very least, it is obviously what one major CRM consulting firm thinks the process is. Why is this?

I don't think it's just that most CRM consultants haven't read the regulations or that they're trying to make their clients believe that compliance with Section 106 requires that they be hired to dig a lot of holes in archeological sites. I believe that the firm is entirely honest in its perception of the process, and in the "Guide" was trying to explain it in words a client can understand. This, of course, is one reason for the discrepancy. Clients, one may argue, don't need to know about the agency's responsibilities, because clients just gotta do what they're told to do by the agencies that have the compliance responsibility. This assumes, of course, that the client isn't itself an agency, but let's stipulate that for the sake of argument.

So if the client isn't an agency, does she or he need to know all the ins and outs of the regulatory process? Arguably not; even certainly not. I can't keep track of the number of times I've heard nonfederal applicants for federal assistance or licenses—and often enough, agency people too—say "Just tell me what to do and I'll do it." They ask, in other words, for the bottom line, unadorned by regulatory fol-de-rol.

But what *is* the bottom line? Surely it matters to a nonfederal client that the agency she's dealing with has to consult a wide range of people and let the public in on what it's doing. Surely it's relevant that all kinds of historic properties and all kinds of effects have to be considered and that APEs have to be defined based on the full range of predicted effects. It might be useful to have some notion about the categories into which such properties and effects tend to fall. Surely it's important to know that the standard for adequacy in identification is only making a "reasonable and good faith effort," not finding every archeological site and digging holes in it.

None of this has made its way into the "Guide," however. So in the view of the firm, and others who share the firm's beliefs about Section 106, such things must not really be important. Never mind that they're what the regulations call for; they are not what anybody's required to do on a day-to-day basis. In what passes for Section 106 compliance for the firm and its colleagues, it must be that people are instead required to do "Phase I, II, and III" fieldwork, to locate every single archeological site that may be affected but not necessarily anything else, to address only direct physical impacts, and to "mitigate" such impacts through either physical avoidance or data recovery.

What and who require them to do this instead of following the regulations? Custom, I suspect; tradition, as expressed by consultants and SHPOs who are comfortable with this way of doing business. But there are at least four other factors at work, I think.

The first of these is the fact that the Advisory Council, the agency responsible for overseeing compliance with its regulations, has almost nothing to do with how most of Section 106 review is carried out on most projects. It's notable that the firm's "Guide" deals almost entirely with the early parts of review—with identification and evaluation. It ignores effect determination altogether and makes only a rather passing reference to how adverse effects are resolved—in its formulation always via physical avoidance or data recovery. The Advisory Council, although its regulations tell agencies how they're supposed to do identification and evaluation, studiously avoids getting involved in these critical operations. These, it holds, are the responsibility of the National Park Service to oversee. NPS thoroughly agrees, but makes little or no effort to inform itself about how identification and evaluation are done by agencies, or to grapple with the real-world problems that agencies face in doing them. In other words, neither of the ostensible oversight agencies involved in Section 106 review supervises or even pays attention to how identification and evaluation are done.

The second factor involved, I believe, has to do with those real-world problems mentioned above. Notable among these is that no agency is really fully staffed to carry out Section 106 review in accordance with the regulations on every one of its projects. SHPOs are no better off and often are even more stressed by fiscal and personnel limitations. Both agencies and SHPOs look for simple, more or less automatic ways to carry out review. Prescribing "Phase I-II-II survey" and avoidance or data recovery can be pretty easily automated.

A third important factor is a product of the history of Section 106 review. Largely because of the way Executive Order 11593 was interpreted to the agencies by NPS back in the 1970s, most agency and SHPO "Section 106 shops" are largely staffed by archeologists, whose primary concerns of course are with archeological sites and the physical impact of projects on such sites.

Finally, there's the fact that for simple, garden-variety federal undertakings that make up most of the workload of agencies, SHPOs, and consultants, it really is overkill to insist on the level of public involvement, open consultation, and attention to all kinds of properties and impacts that are called for by the regulations. The traffic won't bear their routine imposition. When the project is a short segment of sewer line, or a boat dock, or minor widening of a road, there's usually little or no public interest in its impacts, and virtually all of its impacts really are on archeological sites.

Putting all these factors together, I don't think it's a surprise that the traditional way of doing what people think is Section 106 review is the kind of procedure that's described in the "Guide." It's a whole lot easier for an SHPO to say "Do a Phase I survey of the project area" than it is to say "consult with concerned parties, do scoping, and then do what scoping tells you will be a reasonable and good faith effort to identify historic properties in the APE." It's equally easy for an agency, rather than think-ing about the vagaries of public participation, APE definition, and scop-ing, to just say "Do what the SHPO says." It's easy for consultants, once they know the system, to budget for "Phase I surveys." And, in the great majority of cases, nobody is going to care that what's done isn't really in consonance with the regulations.

But there are good reasons that the regulations say what they say and not what the "Guide" says. The public *does* have concerns about impacts on historic properties, which are not all archeological sites (or old build-ings) and which are not affected only by direct physical disturbance. Mul-tiparty consultation *is* required by law.[3] A rigid "find it/assess it/dig it up" (Phase I-II-III) system is not always, or even often, appropriate when one thinks about addressing the full range of effects on the full range of pub-lic interests in the full range of historic properties. It's more than inap-propriate; it's grotesque.

What's needed is a system for dealing with common, garden-variety Section 106 cases that's as easy for SHPOs, agency CRM people, and consultants to practice as is the system outlined in the "Guide," but one that actually meets the requirements of law and addresses the broad pub-lic interest in historic properties. I don't have quite the chutzpah to think that I can sit right here and make up such a system, but I think it's some-thing we ought to work on. What we ought *not* to do is continue as we are, with regulations that tell us to do one thing and a day-to-day practice in which we do something entirely different.

Notes

1. Not its actual exact name.
2. That is, architectural and/or engineering documentation to the standards of the Historic American Buildings Survey/Historic American Engineering Record in the National Park Service.
3. C.f. Section 110(a)(2)(E) of NHPA.

7

What if We Lost Section 106?
Is the Worst Case Necessarily
the Worst Case?

Preface (2002)

In 1994, the Republicans under Newt Gingrich seized control of Congress. There was much alarm in the land of historic preservation. The Advisory Council on Historic Preservation and the Section 106 process were seen as particularly vulnerable to attack, and there was a great rallying around to support them—even by people who were pretty fed up with the Advisory Council and the dithery way it was approaching the adventure in regulatory reform that would lead, five years later, to revised Section 106 regulations.

In this atmosphere of alarm I wrote the following chapter and distributed it via the Internet. It attracted little attention, and was soundly ignored, not only by the Council and its supporters but also by those they feared. I think this is too bad; I actually rather hoped that some radical Republican activist would pick it up and run with it.

So innocent are we of historical perspective that today, only eight years later, nobody in the preservation world seems to remember much about the alarms of 1994—except for those who rather smugly look back and congratulate themselves for fending off another attack by the Evil Ones. I think that this, too, is too bad. The "danger" of losing the Section 106 process should have been the stimulus to some real thinking about alternatives, about what it is that's worth keeping in the process and about what might fruitfully be discarded or changed. About how we might have used the ugly situation to build a better system. It's in the interests of provoking some such debate, at least in isolated corners of the field, that I include the following chapter. It's been suggested that I should "de-historicize" it, bring it up to date somehow, but I disagree. It was a product of its time and is best understood as such. But a time like 1994 may well come again, and if it does, I hope we can be thoughtful enough to treat it as an opportunity for improving the impact assessment system rather than just rally to the defense of an unsatisfactory but familiar status quo.

Introduction (1994)

The National Historic Preservation Act (NHPA) was signed into law in 1966 by Lyndon Baines Johnson, during his creation of the "Great Society." It had been enacted by a Congress whose lower house had for a dozen years been in the hands of the Democratic Party. The same party has remained in control of the House, and often the whole Congress, during the twenty-eight years since. All of the institutions spawned by NHPA—the National Register of Historic Places, the Advisory Council on Historic Preservation, the State Historic Preservation Officers (SHPO), the Section 106 review process—have grown through babyhood and adolescence to stodgy middle age under the kindly if sometimes irascible oversight of a Democratic House of Representatives.

For at least the next two years, we will be living in a different world. As a result, there is fear and trembling in the historic preservation bureaucracy and among the many nonbureaucrats who treasure what the National Historic Preservation program stands for. Many "worst case scenarios" are being spun out. The Advisory Council may be abolished or left to wither without appropriations. Consideration of impacts on historic properties may be limited to those owned by the federal government. The National Register may be gravely constrained in its determinations of eligibility. The SHPOs may become the craven creatures of the governors, with no checks and balances by the Feds. In short, the whole complicated house of cards we have built since 1966 may be blown down by the Big Bad Elephants who are trumpeting about Capitol Hill.

Or maybe not. Maybe they won't get to things as puny as historic preservation before they shoot themselves in the foot and—as they did in 1950 and 1954—lose control after a couple of years. Maybe if we're just quiet and nice and don't make any trouble. . . .

There is already evidence that the "don't make trouble" strategy is being adopted by the preservation bureaucracy. At Mount Shasta in California, the Keeper of the National Register has recently bowed to minor-league political pressure and undone aspects of a perfectly legitimate eligibility determination. It is reported that the Advisory Council will think long and hard before taking a position on an agency-proposed Section 106 agreement that might expose the Council to criticism. It appears that the foes of preservation can have their way with NHPA without raising a finger; preservation's advocates in government will emasculate themselves, because they see no other way to survive.

This reaction is expectable and in a way appropriate for people within the government, wherein preservation of one's program and its dependent personnel is always paramount, regardless of the consequences for the program's ostensible purpose or product. Those of us outside government, though, are free to consider other possibilities. I suggest that such possibilities exist, and that pursuing them may be much preferable to just hunkering down and waiting for the winds of evil to die down.

The focus of this chapter is the Section 106 review process and to a lesser extent the National Register of Historic Places. I have been practicing Section 106 review, boy and man, since 1968; I am a fan of the process. I am not a fan of the National Register, but I have long accepted it as a necessary evil. There is a lot that troubles me about the Section 106 process, however, as it has evolved over the last two and a half decades. The problems with the process have become increasingly clear to me over the last five years, as I've worked with it from the outside on behalf of various clients and concerned citizens and as I've tried to teach about it. I've found it seeming more and more to be a very closed, esoteric system, run by preservationists for preservationists, less and less responsive to the real concerns of real people. Including, if you please, such real people as property owners and developers, to say nothing of Indian tribes, community groups, and minorities. Thus I am led to wonder, first, whether the system we have is so superior that it deserves to be maintained. This in turn leads me to wonder whether, rather than seeking to save what we have, we might be better advised to agree with proposals to scrap it and seek to negotiate something new and better in its place.

We have all heard the proverb about viewing problems as opportunities. Perhaps we should look at a Congress that may well decide to gut processes like Section 106 review as an opportunity to be enjoyed rather than simply as a problem to be contended with, an enemy to be fought. Perhaps we should see it as an opportunity to get back to basics, think through what our real priorities are, and strip away a lot of institutional encumbrances. Perhaps including the Advisory Council, the National Register, and Section 106 itself.

The Basics

What is it we—"we" meaning historic preservationists—seek through Section 106 review? Although in each particular case we have particular interests, our general intent is to ensure that historic properties are given a fair shake in planning. We make much of the fact that Section 106 is not designed to place preservation of such properties above other public interests, and it clearly is not. In simply requiring that agencies "take into account" the effects of their actions on historic properties, Congress signaled that historic properties are to be considered in planning, not that their preservation be elevated above all else. By requiring that agencies seek the comments of the Advisory Council, by giving the Council rulemaking authority, and by establishing certain things that agencies must do (consult with others, etc.) in carrying out Section 106 review, Congress indicated that "taking into account" must mean more than merely giving lip service to historic properties; it involves a rational process of consideration. This is the best that we can—and should, as responsible citizens—seek: balanced consideration of historic preservation interests along with other public interests when planning undertakings in which the federal government is involved.

The Section 106 process as we have all come to know it—the identification of properties that might be eligible for the National Register, their evaluation to determine whether they are eligible, the assessment of effects on those that are eligible, consultation to resolve adverse effects, the execution of Memoranda of Agreement (MOAs), or the rendering of Council comment—is the process that has evolved over the years by which the requirements of Section 106 are carried out. Actually the process sprang virtually full-blown from the head of the Council's first executive director, Bob Garvey, and a small cohort back in the late 1960s and has evolved only by refinement since then. Be this as it may, we've been practicing the standard Section 106 process for the last twenty-seven years or so, occasionally crafting alternatives to it under Programmatic Agreements (PAs). It's worked, on balance, pretty well, though I think its success is a lot more impressive to those who are employed to make it work than to many on whom it has operated. But it is not necessarily the only way to achieve the basic goal of getting due consideration for historic properties. Moreover, I think there are reasons for questioning whether it is the best way.

What's Wrong with Section 106?

A group of archeologists writing in the National Park Service newsletter *CRM* recently commented disparagingly that Native American participation in archeological research under Section 106 and related federal laws "too often has been reduced to a scripted formality codified in PMOAs (Programmatic Memorandum of Agreement)."[1] Section 106 purists may quibble that PMOAs were executed only under the regulations that governed the review process prior to 1986 (they're now called PAs, for Programmatic Agreements). More to the point, it is arguable that an agreement document produced under Section 106 is *supposed to* be "formal," if not "scripted," since it is legally binding on those that sign it. The quote is germane, however, because it reflects a widespread perception of the Section 106 process and the documented agreements it produces—as matters of mere formality, having little to do with reality. This viewpoint is by no means limited to archeologists; in my work I routinely encounter preservationists of every professional stripe, to say nothing of planners, lawyers, bureaucrats, and just plain folk who draft and sign MOAs and PAs that they don't understand and who having signed them file them and go on to do things with and to historic properties that bear only the faintest relationships to what they have signed. MOAs and PAs are drafted in ways that will "please the SHPO," or "get past the Advisory Council," with little concern for how well they reflect the agreement of the consulting parties who sign them. Stipulations are included that are routinely ignored, and actions that have been agreed to are often not represented in the documents. In short, the agreement documents that represent, in theory, the successful completion of review under Section 106 are simply not respected by the parties who draft and presumably implement them. Their "scripted formality" is seen as irrelevant to what happens on the ground, in the real world.

This view of MOAs and PAs reflects a widespread view of the Section 106 process itself as a hoop to be jumped through, rather than as a creative exercise in problem solving. As SHPOs have become increasingly central to the process, the process has come to be viewed as a matter of "getting SHPO clearance," rather than one of constructive consultation. SHPOs, with limited time, funds, and staff and steadily increasing workloads, have opted for stock solutions to problems: If an agency agrees to such a solution—or is willing to sign an agreement document saying that it will adhere to such a solution, whether it really will or not—its project can transit SHPO review with ease. If it attempts something more creative, or is willing to fight for its own point of view, its way will be obstructed—not necessarily because the SHPO wants to be obstructionist, but simply because the SHPO has no time for creativity or discourse.

SHPO attitudes, limitations, and workloads are by no means the only sources of difficulty with the Section 106 process. The process has become increasingly esoteric over the years, increasingly dependent on hair-splitting application of criteria, standards, and procedures, each opaque to the nonspecialist. This makes it subject to unintentional and intentional manipulation by those who *are* specialists. When the applicant for a federal permit is assured by its historic preservation consultant that Section 106 requires conduct of a Phase IIB archeological investigation, or preparation of HABS/HAER documentation, it is a rare applicant who can do anything but scratch its corporate head and write the check. The assurance given by the consultant may have been given in perfectly good faith, because there is little widespread understanding even in professional ranks as to what Section 106 really *does* require. In many states and regions the process has come to be festooned with locally specific requirements and assumptions: procedures promulgated by SHPOs or regional professional organizations; regionally specific terms of art, and assumptions about the roles the Advisory Council, the National Park Service, and other organizations. The situation is not clarified by Advisory Council staff, who are sometimes themselves either less than well informed or deliberately obfuscatory, and by NPS regional offices with their own axes to grind.

Two main groups of people—to say nothing of historic resources—tend to suffer as a result of this procedural opacity. One of these is the group of applicants for federal assistance and federal permits, whose actions are the subjects of Section 106 review. Whipsawed among regulatory agencies, SHPOs, consultants, and sometimes the Council and/or NPS, applicants can wind up spending vast amounts of money, and seeing their projects greatly delayed, in order to do nothing more than—from their (often justified) perspective—make the SHPO happy, enrich a consultant, or produce an MOA that meets "standards" that have little to do with reality.

The second group is the public, notably including those elements of the public that are interested in preserving their cultural environment. Although the Section 106 regulations give lip service to involving the public, in fact the public is involved only to the extent the "core players"—the project agency, the SHPO, and the Council when it is involved—determine to be appropriate. With agencies interested in obtaining prompt "clearance" for their projects, and SHPOs tempted toward project processing by rote in order to avoid being swamped by their workloads, there is little likelihood that the concerned public will be invited into review of a project. If a concerned group does get invited in, or if it discovers that review is underway, its participation is impeded by the same opacity that befuddles the applicant for a permit.

If Section 106 review was ever a process of open consultation among concerned parties, it certainly is not so now. In the great bulk of cases it is a matter of rote "clearance" actions performed bilaterally between agencies and SHPOs. The minority of cases in which consultation does occur tend to be "trouble" cases, in which consultation opens up only after an attempt to achieve clearance has failed. Perhaps a concerned local group forces its way into the process, or is invited in through the action of a concerned agency or SHPO staff person (whose concern, however, may amount to individual axe grinding and hence distort the process). Perhaps an applicant, or an agency, decides to stand up and fight rather than acceding to what it perceives to be unreasonable demands. Whatever the proximate cause, consultation tends to occur in an atmosphere of hostility and misunderstanding. Why *won't* the SHPO give us clearance? What do you mean you don't want to follow the Secretary of the Interior's Standards for Rehabilitation? They're *required!*

Thus Section 106 review has come to be less a matter of reasoned, sensible discourse leading to the resolution of adverse effects on historic properties than one of seeking rote sign-offs and fighting when these are not promptly awarded. Sometimes the "solutions" that result from this process are doubtless good ones from the standpoint of public policy. Even when they are, however, I suggest that the process by which they are reached is one that badly needs fixing. It may not be a process that is worth fighting for if an alternative is available.

At the heart of the problem with Section 106 lie three institutions: the SHPO, the Advisory Council, and the National Register.

As suggested above, I think the SHPO has simply become too pivotal a figure in the Section 106 process. Ironically, Section 106 itself never mentions the SHPO; the SHPO's role in the process is an artifact of the regulations, generally canonized in law by the 1992 amendment to Section 110(a)(2). In the early days of Section 106, when for all practical purposes the SHPOs had the only professional preservation staffs abroad in the land, it was necessary and appropriate to vest them with considerable authority and responsibility. As the years have passed, many major agencies have developed their own preservation staffs and developed their own internal preservation planning systems—albeit at least as much under the authority of the National Environmental Policy Act as under that of NHPA. A quarter-century of environmental impact review has conditioned federal agencies and the state, local, and private recipients of their assistance and licenses to the notion that effects on the environment, including the cultural environment, should be considered in planning their actions. In short, although there are certainly exceptions, federal agencies and those they work with are far more equipped today than they were twenty years ago to consider the effects of their actions on historic properties. Ironically, though, the evolution of the Section 106 process has been to place more and more responsibility on the SHPO not only to advise and counsel but also literally to dictate to agencies about preservation requirements. As discussed above, this has placed such pressures on the SHPOs that they have tended to opt for strategies that apply lowest-common-denominator solutions to all preservation problems. As for the agencies, many of them have been quite satisfied to let the SHPOs do their work for them. Why build competence in preservation, or consider creative solutions to problems, if all one really has to do is satisfy the SHPO?

The Council seems to be having great difficulty figuring out what its role in Section 106 review will be, or indeed whether it should even have one. In a few instances, mostly in the west, the Council has made real efforts to open up the process to nongovernmental interests, notably those of Indian tribes and applicants for federal permits, but for the most part it seems to have resigned itself to the role of rubber stamp for "solutions" arrived at by agencies and SHPOs. Its revised draft regulations do nothing but formalize this role, while attempting to craft a questionable new role as an appellate body. An entity is needed to oversee and coordinate Section 106 review, but the Council is well on its way toward abrogating its own performance of this role.

The National Register's role in the unworkability of Section 106 review is more subtle, and in a way more interesting, than that of either the Council or the SHPO. The problem with the Register, I believe, is that it seeks to serve two different, conflicting purposes. One purpose is essentially commemorative, to identify those properties that should be preserved because they commemorate or illustrate some aspect of history at the national, state, or local level. The second purpose is to serve as a planning tool, identifying those properties that should be considered in planning federal, federally assisted, federally licensed, and presumably other undertakings. The party line is that these purposes do not really conflict, because the second effectively means that preservation should be considered. In fact, there is a very fundamental, conceptual conflict: Commemoration is forever; consideration is for *now*.

A property that is good for *commemoration* will always be good for commemoration, as long as it survives intact. That is inherent in the commemorative exercise. It follows that it should be protected in perpetuity, using all the legal tools at the government's disposal. This implies that we are willing to commit the property to preservation, and not to anything else, and this of course has serious implications in terms of the property's use and its commercial value. A property (or anything else) may be worthy of *consideration* today, at this moment, even though it was not worthy in the past, and may not be worthy in the future. It may be worthy of consideration even if nobody has any intention of preserving it in perpetuity. It may be worthy of consideration even if it has no commemorative value at all. A family farm that will be bisected by a new highway may have great emotional value to its owners and their neighbors, even though it will inevitably be swallowed up by suburban development within the next generation. A Native American sacred site may be vital to the integrity of a tribe's culture, but have to be kept secret so it cannot possibly be used to commemorate anything. A very ordinary archeological site—one of a million similar sites—may be able to provide scholarship with a little bit of useful information if it is studied before it is destroyed. A World War II gun emplacement may be duplicated by a dozen others, some of which are better candidates for the commemoration of World War II, and still be worthy of documentation before it is destroyed. In short, consideration is a much broader concept than commemoration, and it is one whose practical concomitants are much more varied.

Confusion between commemoration and consideration accounts for many of the silly, time-consuming, and often damaging arguments that arise about eligibility for the National Register. If one thinks of the Register as a commemorative tool, then it follows that only the "best and the brightest" of properties should be included. It also follows that every reasonable effort should be made, by governments at all levels and by citizens everywhere, to preserve each such property. This being the case, it also follows that the Register needs to be very discriminating not only about what it allows to be regarded as eligible but also about how each such entity is documented. The objectively defined historical significance of a property must be demonstrated if we expect resources to be expended on its long-term preservation. Its boundaries must be very carefully defined because they will have long-term land-use implications; what's inside should be preserved, what's outside need not be. If one thinks of the Register as an indicator of what must be considered in planning, then an inclusive Register makes sense, one that includes not just the "best and brightest," but all places that have historical interest. This is sensible because consideration does not imply that long-term preservation is always appropriate or desirable; no extraordinary efforts are expected on behalf of a property's preservation simply because it is eligible for the Register. Accordingly, there is little need to get deeply involved in scholarly arguments about significance or in hair-splitting about boundaries.

On a day-to-day basis, the Section 106 process uses the National Register Criteria as the bases for deciding what needs to be considered in planning. As long as everybody plays along, rather fast and loose, with the Criteria, they work pretty well. But when a question arises, and the various guidelines for applying the Criteria are consulted—and whenever an issue is referred to the Keeper of the Register for a determination of eligibility—then people start looking at the subject property through the lens of commemoration. This is because the National Register, logically enough, wants to apply precisely the same standards and guidelines to eligibility determinations that it does to nominations. The primary rationale for nominating anything to the National Register is to commemorate its significance, so the pertinent standards and guidelines are designed with a commemoration model in mind.

The practical result of all this is that people can spend large amounts of time and money debating whether a given property is eligible for the Register, with the arguments focusing largely on issues that make sense in the context of a commemoration model but no sense at all in terms of consideration. A wise agency will consider whatever concerned members of the public think is worthy of consideration; if it is of concern to the public, it is an aspect of the environment that ought to be addressed. When an effort is made to cast these concerns in National Register terms, however, then we quickly become embroiled in contentions about whether the property in question is one of the best and the brightest, whether it merits preservation in perpetuity, what its precise boundaries are, and so forth. These arguments can lead to great frustration by all concerned. Members of the public who are concerned about a property feel that their interests are being subordinated to those of a bunch of unfeeling federal bureaucrats with a lot of arbitrary rules and regulations. Those who want to get on with a project despite opposition from preservation interests feel that the law is being misused in a pretence that some diddly little house or site or landscape is the equivalent of Mt. Vernon.

Another important bedevilment that arises from the confusion between commemoration and consideration models results from the way the Register tends to be used by nonfederal government entities. Local governments have traditionally designated historic properties—notably historic districts—for commemorative purposes, with the intention of preserving them over the long term. State and local governments have more authority than the federal government does to regulate the behavior of individual citizens, and the intellectual tradition of local-level historic preservation especially is one that features a high level of control. The traditional means of carrying out historic preservation at the local level is through the formal designation of local historic districts and the empanelment of preservation commissions with a great deal of control over what happens in the districts for which they are responsible. Live in a locally designated district and you will find yourself unable to change the windows in your home, perhaps cut trees in your front yard, perhaps paint the façade, or even put up a political campaign poster without leave from the historic district commission. When a state or local government adopts its own preservation laws or regulations, it typically builds in some kind of control along the lines suggested by the historic district commission tradition. Even if it doesn't—even if its law does little more than echo the consideration model that is expressed by Section 106—people are likely to assume that "historical designation" means a great deal of government control over individual behavior.

Naturally, the National Park Service encourages state and local governments to use the National Register and its criteria to identify properties worthy of preservation. The status of the Register as a commemorative device recommends it for such use. As a result, it is not uncommon for state and local governments to enact laws protecting National Register–eligible properties. These laws may be much more intrusive upon the actions of private citizens than Section 106 could ever be.

The result is obvious: A determination of eligibility, made under Section 106 for the sole purpose of identifying a property that a federal agency should consider in its planning, becomes the trigger for a whole range of protective requirements imposed by a state or local government, based on a commemoration model that justifies a high level of preservation and a kind of police power that only states and local governments can wield. Under such circumstances the determination of eligibility cannot be a planning tool; it becomes a political act.

I have belabored the role of the National Register partly because it is the most complicated of those I've tried to discuss and partly because it is the most intrinsic to the Section 106 process. The problems with Section 106 will not be cured by tinkering with the Advisory Council's regulations or by giving the Council new authorities or new leadership. The bottom line is that the Section 106 process, and the institutions that make it run, may not be worth saving. Rather than fighting rear-guard actions to save them, or to save them in bits and pieces or in forms even more emasculated than they are at present, we may be well advised to look at alternatives.

An Alternative

Assuming that our purpose, as discussed above, is simply to ensure that historic properties are fairly considered in planning, what alternatives are there to Section 106 review as we have known it this last quarter-century? I suggest that we look toward the review of federal projects under the National Environmental Policy Act (NEPA).

Why, the reader may ask, should we imagine that NEPA will survive when Section 106 may not? Primarily because the basic idea of analyzing the environmental effects of projects, as NEPA requires, has become pretty well ingrained both in agency planning processes and in the American psyche over the last couple of decades. Indeed, environmental impact assessment has become an institution in all the world's developed nations and in many less developed countries. NEPA also lacks the internal contradictions that Section 106's intimate relationships with the National Register create. NEPA is a pure "consideration" authority; it makes no claim to identify resources for long-term preservation or management, and hence it does not appear to conflict with the private ownership and management of land in the way Section 106 appears to because of its connections with the National Register.

I assume, then, that we will continue to have a NEPA review process, in more or less its current form. At the moment, NEPA analyses typically do not treat historic properties, or the cultural environment generally, very well.[2] In large measure, however, this results from the very fact that Section 106 review exists. Agencies tend to give "cultural resources" short shrift in the NEPA process because they assume such resources will be taken care of through "mitigation" worked out under Section 106. If we were confronted with an attempt to do away with Section 106, we might very well negotiate an improvement in the way the cultural environment is dealt with under NEPA.

How would historic preservation review work without Section 106? Perhaps like this:

First, the review system should be divorced from the National Register. Let the Register be the Register, do what the Register does best—that is, serve as a tool for commemoration. Let it be as broad or narrow, as inclusive or exclusive, as it wishes, or as the traffic will bear. Focus the review system on the cultural environment—that is, those aspects of the physical and social environments that are determined through a NEPA analysis to have, or express, cultural value *at the time the analysis is performed.* The cultural environment would of course include National Register properties, and some criteria (not necessarily those of the National Register) would have to be employed to evaluate nonregistered properties, but it would also include other places perceived to have cultural significance, as well as nonplace social institutions and lifeways. There would be no implication that any aspect of the cultural environment as defined in a NEPA analysis would have permanent status as an officially designated significant thing; each such aspect would simply be identified as something to be considered, like the current quality of the water and the current state of soil erosion.

Agencies would need to analyze the lists of project types that they currently regard as categorically excluded from NEPA review (CX or CatEx projects), to make sure that each had little potential to do damage to the cultural environment. Such review would doubtless be resisted by some agencies, but it need not result in vast changes in CX lists, particularly if "conditional" CXs could be included. Interior remodeling of a federal building, for example, could surely be a CX on the condition that it be done according to appropriate rehabilitation standards. The idea would be to discriminate between routine projects having little potential to generate public concern on cultural grounds and nonroutine projects that have greater potential for generating such concern. The former would be handled in house following relevant standards, the latter subjected to further analysis and outside review.

For projects requiring further review—essentially those that today require an environmental assessment (EA) or environmental impact statement (EIS), the agency would identify concerned parties (as is done today) and initiate consultation (as is not necessarily done today under NEPA). Consultation would be one part of the agency's analysis of environmental effects, which would be required to include analysis of:

- effects on elements of the cultural environment, including historic places;

- alternatives to avoid or mitigate adverse effects; and

- the concerns of interested parties, including but not limited to historical and cultural concerns, economic concerns, and property concerns.

The agency would seek to reach agreement with interested parties. If agreement was reached, the agency would document the agreement and proceed in accordance with its terms. If agreement was not reached, the agency would prepare a record of decision explaining the basis for its decision to proceed without agreement. This decision would be subject to appeal through processes established within each agency and ultimately through referral to the Council on Environmental Quality (CEQ) as is the case under NEPA today.

The idea, in short, would be to blend the major strength of the Section 106 process—the idea of consultation to reach binding agreements—with the strengths of the NEPA process—its emphasis on objective analysis and agency responsibility. This would be done without requiring a structured role for SHPOs, without a focus on the National Register, and without an Advisory Council. The Register would be left to serve as a commemorative tool, and the SHPOs would continue to coordinate historic preservation programs in their states. The Advisory Council could either continue as a general policy advisor to the president and Congress or be disbanded, with its program review and educational functions shifting to CEQ.

Conclusion

Two things have motivated me to offer the thoughts, and particularly the recommendations, above. First, I fear that the reaction of the preservation community to the assaults that must come on the Section 106 process from the new Congress will be to allow the process to be nibbled away—or even to slice off chunks and toss them to the sharks in the hope of stemming a feeding frenzy. This will result in a Section 106 process that continues to support an infrastructure but fails to perform the basic task of ensuring that historic properties, broadly defined, are considered in planning. The second motivation is my increasingly strong belief that the

Section 106 process is already failing in its performance of that task, because it has become too bogged down in procedure and too compromised by its relationship to the National Register.

I suggest that rather than waiting for attacks to come and then trying to fend them off through piecemeal reaction, we seek consensus on a desired state toward which to negotiate and then negotiate toward it as the attacks come. The above is my first attempt to formulate a desired state and a negotiating position. The position is, in essence, to give up the Advisory Council, the existing Section 106 process, and the idea of the National Register as all things to all people, in favor of integrating the best parts of the Section 106 process into the procedures for NEPA review.

Of course, things are never so orderly that the preservation community, even if it were to achieve consensus on a negotiating direction, would be given the opportunity to pursue it in an orderly manner. In all probability the attacks on the Section 106 process, when they come, will not be frontal; they will be nibbling sorts of things on the flanks. The most direct attacks, in fact, will probably not be on the Advisory Council and Section 106 itself; they will be on the National Register and the procedures employed in making eligibility determinations. Assaults on the Council will probably come through the appropriations process. Even in these disorderly contexts, though, there may be opportunities to negotiate a more comprehensive solution to the problems the Congress is likely to perceive with Section 106. Moreover, before congressional pressure begins, or at least before it gathers steam, the administration itself is likely to be looking for agencies to cut and regulations to simplify. This could provide a context in which to offer helpful proposals.

I realize that some readers will brand what I have written as anathema and see me as something of a traitor to the cause to have even offered the above thoughts as a possibility. I realize that it goes against a lot of grains to suggest, in effect, giving up whole institutions when we might be able to get away with only marginal losses. My fear, though, is that the marginal losses will not really be so marginal; they will instead cut at the very heart of what makes Section 106 review worth doing. Conversely, my belief is that the institutions it is our knee-jerk response to protect may not be all that worth protecting.

The next two years are likely to be precarious times for the historic preservation community, and particularly for those elements of the community that derive much of their identity from Section 106. I strongly believe that the way to live in such times is to try to make the most of them, rather than seeking to maintain the status quo. Now that the asteroid has struck, we would be smarter to be mammals than dinosaurs.

Notes

1. Sullivan, Hanson, and Hawkins 1994.
2. See King and Rafuse 1994.

8

What's in a Name? The Case of "Potentially Eligible" Historic Properties

> The proposed project will have no effect on National Register of Historic Places eligible or potentially eligible properties."[1]

What's wrong with the above quote? Most cultural resources consultants and SHPOs would probably say "nothing," provided there's a factual basis for the determination of "no effect." In fact, though, there *is* a problem—with use of the term "potentially eligible."

This term (seldom formally defined) is widely used in Section 106–related reports and other documents to mean "not yet evaluated property that may meet the National Register Criteria." We need to have a term to use in referring to such properties. But "potentially eligible" is an unfortunate choice.

Webster[2] defines "potential" as "that which can, but has not yet, come into being . . . as opposed to *actual*." So a "potentially eligible" property must be one that has *not yet met* the National Register Criteria—not one that may meet them but hasn't yet been found to do so. In fact, if we follow Webster, a "potentially eligible property" is not *actually* eligible at all.

I know, I know, I'm quibbling, picking a nit. But I also know where the devil resides.

Section 106 requires agencies to take into account the effects of their actions on properties included in or eligible for inclusion in the National Register. If a "potentially eligible" property's eligibility "has not yet come into being," if it's not "actually" eligible, then clearly—at least at the time it's described, it's *not* eligible. Its eligibility may somehow come into being at some later date, but you could say that about any piece of real property. Something could happen to my back yard tomorrow—an alien spaceship landing, the assassination of some (badly misplaced) dignitary—that would make it eligible. All property is potentially eligible. But a *potentially* eligible property by definition is not *presently* eligible for the National Register. Section 106 requires the consideration of impacts only on properties that are on or eligible for the Register—not properties that may hypothetically become eligible at some point in the future.

Obviously, the fact that a place might someday become eligible though it's not so right now is not what cultural resource specialists mean when they say a property is potentially eligible. They mean that it *may* be eligible *right now,* but they don't know yet whether it is. It needs more work before they can be sure whether or not it meets the National Register Criteria and merits more consideration.

Unfortunately, while cultural resource specialists may know that they don't really mean, literally, that a potentially eligible property currently isn't eligible but might become so in the future, others—for instance, lawyers and judges—may very well assume that they mean what the dictionary suggests they mean. Indeed, some attorneys have recently voiced precisely that assumption to me, as a rationale for arguing that the Section 106 regulations illegally extend review to impacts on properties beyond those that Congress had in mind when it enacted NHPA. Their argument, if successful, would take us back to the bad old days when you had to get a formal determination of eligibility from the Keeper of the Register before addressing impacts on a place under Section 106. Or even to the worse old days before Executive Order 11593, when agencies weren't responsible for considering impacts on anything that someone else hadn't identified and nominated to the National Register.

The lawyers are wrong, of course, and there's a logical disconnect in their argument—careless use of words like "potentially" really isn't relevant to what they think inaccurately to be the question—whether Congress intended the word "eligible" to mean "eligible" or "determined eligible." But common employment of the "potentially eligible" terminology helps them make their case, at least by generating confusion.

Think about how people use, and don't use, "potential" in other aspects of life. Consider a federal program to provide financial assistance to people with incomes below the officially established poverty line. If we don't know someone's income, but think he or she may be poor, we don't say that he or she is "potentially in poverty," but that she or he "may be" in poverty, subject to further study. After all, everyone is potentially in poverty; all one has to do is lose all one's money. Or imagine a program of health benefits for pregnant women. A woman who applies for the program either is or is not pregnant; tests have to be carried out (or time has to elapse) in order to determine whether she is actually pregnant. When she applies and we're not sure of her condition, we don't say that she's "potentially pregnant"—all healthy women of childbearing age are potentially pregnant. We say she may be pregnant, subject to testing. We wouldn't extend poverty benefits to everyone who is "potentially in poverty," nor pregnancy benefits to everyone who is "potentially pregnant," so why should we extend consideration under Section 106 to properties that are "potentially eligible"?

What the regulations do, in fact, as they have in one way or another since the 1970s in perfect harmony with the statute and Executive Order 11593, is require review of impacts on properties that meet the National Register Criteria—not just to those that someone has formally determined to meet the Criteria. Figuring out whether the Criteria are met is a necessary part of the process, just as establishing someone's income level or childbearing condition would be necessary to processes of poverty assistance or aid to expectant mothers. Just as a person really is or is not poor, just as a woman really is or is not pregnant, a property really is or is not eligible—that is, it either does or does not meet the Register Criteria. The process of determining whether a property is eligible no more *makes* a property eligible than ascertaining someone's income level makes him or her poor. But when we use the term "potentially" as we do, we're strongly implying that a property is *not* eligible until it's formally so determined—thus supporting the notion that officially unevaluated properties are entitled to no consideration.

What to do about this? We should refer to properties whose eligibility isn't certain the same way we refer to people whose income or pregnancy aren't certain—as properties that may be eligible but need further study to allow us to decide whether they really are.

Pretty complicated terminology, I imagine the reader grumbling; it's a lot more convenient to use a simple word like "potentially." Well, sure, but there are a lot of simple terms that we don't use because they have problematical implications. A one-word traditional white person's term for "African American," for example, and a traditional frontiersman's simple term for "Native American woman." We don't use those terms because they're insulting, but we shouldn't use words that are misleading, either. "Potentially eligible" is misleading; something like "may be eligible; needs more investigation" isn't.

But what if we don't want to do more investigation, but instead want to extend some sort of agreed-upon treatment to properties that may be eligible, without explicitly determining them eligible? It's easy to say we'll "follow the Secretary of the Interior's Standards for the Treatment of Historic Properties for all eligible and potentially eligible properties"; or we'll "flag and avoid impacts on all eligible and potentially eligible properties." What do we say if we don't have the "potentially eligible" category?

Well, one thing to think about is this: If we don't know enough to know whether the place is eligible, do we know enough to prescribe treatment? I've personally been on both sides of that question, and I think there are certainly cases in which we don't have to know much at all about a property (or group or type of properties) in order to prescribe treatment. But there are other cases in which we assume too easily that we know enough. The "flag and avoid" strategy is an example—archeologists often assume that if they just put flags around a place and make sure the bulldozers stay outside the flags, they've not only physically avoided the place, but also avoided adverse effects on it. This assumption requires that one know that the place doesn't have qualities that can be compromised by visual, auditory, and other effects that are not direct and physical in nature, and in fact those who rely on "flag and avoid" often don't know this. I don't mean to argue here for elaborate determinations of eligibility in each case—far from it—but I do think we need to know enough about a place to manage impacts on it. Using easy terms like "potentially eligible" can mask failure to give a place's qualities the consideration we need to give them in order to plan effective treatment.

But if we really do need a nonmisleading term to replace "potentially eligible property"—and I don't doubt that we often do—here are some suggestions:

"Property that may be eligible";

"Property that may meet the National Register Criteria";

"Property presumed eligible for purposes of this (agreement, analysis, etc.)";

"Probably eligible property"; or

"Possibly eligible property."

Or, be explicit about the kind of thing you're talking about, without assigning it to an abstract category:

"Buildings over forty-five years of age";

"Flake scatters";

"Landscapes with evidence of Amish farming"; or

"Areas identified by the tribe as culturally sensitive."

At some point in a report or other document, you may have to explain why you're regarding a type of property as likely enough to be eligible for the Register to make some sort of management appropriate under NHPA. Once you've done it, though ("We regard flake scatters as eligible for the National Register because collectively they can provide important information on the behavior of prehistoric flakes"), you can then just refer to the thing as what it is, rather than giving it an abstract collective designator. Of course, your client or the SHPO or somebody else in the 106 process may not want to assume that all flake scatters are eligible; in that case, it's going to be necessary to get more data.

These are surely sufficient words to the wise. If we are to make our words convey what we intend, we have to use them with some precision, and consider their potential—yes, what *might be* even if it *doesn't yet exist*—for generating misunderstanding or being misused.

Notes

1. From a 1999 Section 106 agreement that will remain nameless.

2. *Webster's New Twentieth Century Dictionary of the English Language,* Unabridged 2d ed., Collins World, 1975, p. 1409.

In the Eye of the Beholder: Visual Impacts and Section 106 Review

As this is written, there is much hue and cry in the world of CRM about telecommunications towers. One of the characteristics that all such towers share is that they stick up into the air; as a result, visual impact is a big issue during review under Section 106. Telecom companies, SHPOs, and consultants alike seem to have great difficulty dealing with such impacts. Telecom companies complain that they are being "required" to fund excessively expensive surveys to identify historic properties within expansive areas of potential effect (APEs) as a result of the assumed potential for visual impact. SHPOs respond that it is, after all, the responsibility of the Federal Communications Commission (FCC) to identify historic properties within the APE of each project it may license, reflecting all kinds of potential impact—which means, in the absence of FCC attention to its duty, that it's the applicant company's responsibility. Many CRM contractors find themselves caught in the middle.

It strikes me that in this case, as in many others, much of the problem arises from our understanding of Section 106 review as a rigid progression through discrete steps. First we establish the APE, then we identify, then we evaluate, then we consider effects, and so on. If we were to think of the process as being rather more organic, each of its components influenced by feedback from others, we might approach the matter more reasonably.

Visual impacts cannot exist in the absence of eyes. In fact, it's impossible to have a visual impact on a historic property per se. Visual impacts occur on people looking at, or out from, historic properties (among other places).

More than mere eyeballs are required, however. There have to be brains that interpret the signals that come racing along the optic nerve and to categorize them as representing something offensive, something that has a negative impact. If the brains involved don't so categorize the stimuli they receive, then there cannot be a visual impact.

It follows that visual impacts exist only when people who see the possibly impacting facility *believe* that there are visual impacts. In most cases these are people who live in the vicinity of the proposed facility, or who visit there.

From this it follows that it's thoroughly irrelevant to do architectural surveys of visual APEs—or at least it's irrelevant until it's been established that somebody in or around the APE may be offended by what the facility does to his or her view. It should go without saying that archeological surveys are irrelevant; archeological sites can't see. Things like wireless towers may impact archeological sites, but only within very small areas where their construction physically disturbs the ground.

Every telecommunications company with a brain in its corporate head is concerned about its image in the community in which it operates. That image is obviously affected by the extent to which the community thinks the company respects its character, its uniqueness, the things that make it special. Therefore, telecommunications companies have very good, solid, business reasons to be concerned about visual impacts and to invest money in minimizing or mitigating them—but only when the visual impacts are real impacts on real people. The only reason a telecom company has for considering "impacts" that real people don't perceive or object to is that some screwball law or pompous bureaucrat requires it to.

So it seems to me that the first question that needs to be asked about visual impacts is: Does anyone care? Is there anyone in or around the APE who's likely to be offended by the visual character of the proposed facility? Ascertaining that fact is something that any wise company ought to do simply as a matter of good community relations. If nobody gives a damn, then there's simply no reason to consider such impacts further. If people do care, then it may be appropriate to figure out whether their concerns involve historic properties. Do the concerned people live in an eligible district, or eligible houses; do they ascribe cultural value to an eligible traditional cultural property? Or maybe not; it may be simpler all around just to assume that the places involved are eligible and get on with resolving effects on them under Section 106.

In other words, the first and most important kind of visual impact assessment should be something that a wise company does anyway—find out whether there are people out there who'll be offended by its action. If there are, and only if there are, then architectural (and/or historical, landscape, TCP) surveys may be appropriate and may be understandable by telecom executives as rational investments.

Assessing visual impacts in such a way is not very compatible with a standardized step-by-step approach to Section 106 review—particularly when such review focuses on the "resources" (i.e., buildings, sites, landscapes, etc.) involved rather than on the people who look at or out from them. In standard Section 106 review we first identify the potentially affected properties and then assess effects, and neither enterprise typically involves much effort to ascertain how people (other than preservation professionals) feel about the effects. Doing it by standard steps guarantees that the process will appear stupid, arbitrary, and capricious to the companies that must pay the bill.

Another thing that's worth discussion is the fact that visual impacts are often rather transitory.[1] Telecom towers are a good example; it's thoroughly predictable that within a decade or two—three at the most, surely—technological advance will have made such towers obsolete, and we'll be engaged in bitter arguments about whether taking them down has impacts on the visual character of communities that have come to treasure them. The transitory character of visual impacts isn't limited to such towers. A few years ago I was asked to help with a case involving the visual impacts of a surface mine on a property several miles away. The mine followed a mineral seam around the face of a ridge. As the mining progressed, the scar was filled and planted; within five or six years it would be invisible from the place where impacts were anticipated. But the Criteria of Adverse Effect (36 CFR 800.5(a)) don't take time into account; visual impacts, like physical impacts, are treated as though they're forever. Sometimes they pretty much are, of course, but not always; we ought to have a way of dealing differently with those that aren't. We ought at least to be willing to enter into pretty easy Memoranda of Agreement where only transitory impacts (of any kind) are involved. Assessing and addressing impacts that will surely be gone in a short time should not be as complex as doing so for impacts that are going to hang around for a long time—except where the short-term impact is devastating on, say, the economy of a historic district or the ability of a traditional community to use a spiritual place. One of the first cases reviewed under Section 106, in the late 1960s, was an example of such an exceptional instance. The case involved the potential impacts of a proposed power plant on one side of the Hudson River, on Saratoga Battlefield on the other side. The impact in this case would have been very long term; the plant wasn't going to go away anytime in the foreseeable future. And the property involved was (and is) visited by people who would certainly take offense at a power plant in the viewshed. But this is the exception that proves the rule. The great bulk of visual impact cases do not involve such permanent facilities as powerplants, nor do they involve properties like interpreted battlefields, where the people who value the properties will certainly find the impact offensive.

The Section 106 process was invented in the course of early cases like that of Saratoga Battlefield, so it naturally reflects the character of such cases. Over the decades it has become routinized, standardized, and rigid, and its practitioners have come to believe that the standard way is the only way. It shouldn't be, but it is certainly a fact that the regulations as they're currently written, and interpreted by SHPOs and other routine users, do not make it easy to flex the system to accommodate the realities of things like the visual effects of telecommunications towers. A wireless industry group recently asked me what I thought might be done to flex the system along the lines I've suggested above, and I could only offer the usual, unsatisfactory, idea of a Programmatic Agreement. Programmatic Agreements are the primary system-flexing devices that the regulations offer us, but they are hard and time-consuming to negotiate, particularly when they involve looking at properties and impacts in a way that most Section 106 practitioners find unfamiliar. There ought to be another way, but short of a regulatory change,[2] I'm not sure what it might be.[3]

Notes

1. I'm indebted to Sherman Banker of the Wisconsin SHPO for pointing out this fact to me.

2. For one thing, the Federal Communications Commission could revise its NEPA regulation, which forces telecommunication companies to conduct substantial general environmental assessments whenever there is an "effect" on historic properties. This naturally causes companies to seek to find no historic properties in the viewsheds of their projects, which in turn causes SHPOs to dig in their heels and insist on expansive surveys, and around and around we go.

3. Since writing this chapter, I've worked with colleagues in the Bureau of Land Management, Fish and Wildlife Service, and California and Iowa SHPO offices to explore an alternative that we're provisionally calling an "Identification Agreement," in which an agency enters into an agreement with an SHPO or THPO about what constitutes an appropriate identification effort under particular circumstances. Such an agreement (discussed in the National Preservation Institute's Section 106 Advanced Review classes) might be used to crack the telecom tower/visual impact nut.

10

"Preservation's Responsibility" and Section 4(f) of the Department of Transportation Act

S ection 4(f) of the U.S. Department of Transportation Act[1]—the act creating the Department of Transportation (DOT), enacted on the same day in 1966 that saw the National Historic Preservation Act become reality—forbids "use" of parks, wildlife refuges, and "historic sites" for DOT and DOT-assisted projects if there is any "prudent and feasible alternative" to such use. This is a pretty high standard to meet and requires a lot of detailed, expensive, planning.

The courts have found that when Section 4(f) refers to "historic sites," it means places included in or eligible for the National Register of Historic Places—the same range of properties covered by Section 106 of NHPA. Thus, while most federal agencies have only Section 106 (and the various other cultural resource authorities) to worry about when they need to muck up a historic property, transportation agencies have Section 4(f) as well. Under which they can't get away simply with "taking effects into account" as they do under Section 106; they have to demonstrate that there's no prudent and feasible way to avoid mucking them up.

Which is a good thing, right? Most historic preservationists, knees jerking properly, say "sure." The higher the standard the bastards have to meet before they can sacrifice our heritage on the altar of internal combustion, the better. Section 106 is far too wimpy; Section 4(f) provides real protection.

Transportation officials, just as predictably, feel otherwise. They've let their voices be heard a number of times since the DOT Act became law. Most recently, early in 2001, the American Association of State Highway and Transportation Officials (AASHTO) testified before Congress that the reference to historic sites should be removed from Section 4(f).

The National Trust for Historic Preservation, inviting preservationists to a conference on transportation issues in September of the same year, commented that "the testimony makes it clear that AASHTO is presently convinced that historic preservation regulatory reviews are duplicative and unnecessarily time consuming." In response, the Trust suggested, "It will be historic preservation's responsibility at this conference to explain the integrity of historic preservation reviews and why they are so necessary."

Well, maybe, but if this means that it's the preservation community's responsibility to fight to keep National Register eligible properties in 4(f), I beg to be excused. I think AASHTO's right.

The alert reader may have noted my strong belief that it is simple-minded to try to use the National Register as both an honor role and a planning tool. The real-world results of Section 4(f) protection of historic properties comprise a classic example of why this is so.

Since Congress put historic places on a par with wildlife refuges and parks in Section 4(f), it obviously was thinking of such places as being somewhat alike. The distinguishing features of parks and wildlife refuges, in a property-law sense, are that they have been formally designated as suitable for conservation (or recreation, in the case of some parks) purposes and are set aside as such. Someone—a government, perhaps a government/nongovernment partnership—has invested money, political capital, or other valuables (e.g., land) in setting aside the property to serve that purpose. Some historic places fall into the same kind of category. An example is a locally designated historic district where the local government imposes design controls; another might be a house museum; another a battlefield that has been acquired and interpreted for the public. But of course, such properties make up only a miniscule percentage of the population of places that are included in or eligible for the National Register. A property is eligible for the Register if it meets the National Register Criteria; it doesn't matter whether anybody is willing to invest a nickel or a half hour toward its preservation.

Section 106 explicitly deals with the full range of Register-eligible properties, but it extends to such properties only the "protection" of being "taken into account" in planning. This, I think, is as it should be. Every place with historical associations, every archeological site, every reasonably well preserved piece of vernacular architecture, every place that's ascribed cultural value by a community, should be "taken into account" and not thoughtlessly destroyed. But it's a tremendous distortion of priorities to require that no such place be disturbed if there is any prudent and feasible way to do otherwise.

It's a distortion of public interest priorities in general, and of historic preservation priorities in particular. Here's why.

Consider Highway 106, which runs through Rustbelt City. The highway follows the old stage road along which the city grew up. On the east side of the highway is a cluster of old warehouses—not particularly good warehouses for any modern use, and nobody really cares much about them, but they reflect the history of buglight manufacture, which was important in the city's growth. On the west side of the highway is a neighborhood made up of inexpensive houses built in the 1960s and 1970s, most of them homes to low-income Hispanic families struggling to catch up with the American dream. A stable, hard-working neighborhood made up of people who help one another achieve their goals for their families, their community, and themselves.

Transportation pressures are such that it's necessary to improve traffic flow through Rustbelt City. The city lies in a narrow canyon; it's not feasible to route a new highway around it. Other options—light rail, a tunnel, dirigibles, bicycles—are equally infeasible.

The warehouses are obviously eligible for the National Register; any fool can plainly see that they constitute a district that meets National Register Criterion "a," and maybe "c" as well.[2] The Hispanic neighborhood is almost certainly not eligible; its buildings are too recent, too ordinary, its history is too short. So under Section 4(f) what gets preserved and what gets destroyed? It's obviously feasible and prudent to preserve the warehouses; all one has to do is relocate half the Hispanic neighborhood and knock down their houses. Maybe the neighborhood and its struggling residents can survive this impact and continue to thrive, but maybe they can't. Whether they can or can't, their fate is less important than the fate of a bunch of old warehouses that nobody much cares about—which may get demolished next year to make way for a new Gross-Mart.

There are plenty of examples of this kind of public interest travesty.

Wetlands, woodlands, scenic vistas, low-income neighborhoods, are sacrificed to allow transportation planners to avoid taking historic properties, regardless of their importance or relevance to modern life. Highways wind up with funny (but expensive to construct) bends and curves where historic properties were avoided but then destroyed by somebody else, because no one really much wanted to keep them.

That's the kind of thing that makes Section 4(f) a nightmare from the standpoint of overall public policy, the general public good. In terms of historic preservation it's not much better, whatever knee-jerk protectionists may say.

Transportation planners naturally seek ways to avoid applying Section 4(f) to their projects. This isn't necessarily because they secretly want to pave the world; it may well be that they just don't want to build projects that wipe out neighborhoods or wetlands to protect old buildings. But what can they do? The language of Section 4(f) is pretty blunt. Naturally, strategies do develop, and some of them are pretty bad for the integrity of historic preservation review.

One strategy has been to argue, in essence, that if a property—usually an archeological site—is important only for the research one can do there, then one hasn't really used or destroyed the property if one bulldozes it into oblivion, as long as one first recovers the important research information the property contains. In other words, if you do archeology you don't have to do 4(f), provided the place is significant only for research. And how do we know whether this is all it's significant for? Easy: If it's found eligible under National Register Criterion "d"—if it has produced or may produce information significant in history or prehistory—then obviously its good only for research and it can be blown away. So transportation planners may lean very hard on their consultants, and on SHPOs, to find properties eligible only under Criterion "d," ignoring their associational values (Criteria "a" and "b") and their significance as examples of types, styles, works of masters, and so on (Criterion "c"). Reaching this sort of conclusion may require use of a careful "See no evil, hear no evil" strategy—limit the people you talk with and the people who know about the project, because they might bring up something that conflicts with the conclusion to which you're predisposed.

Even better than using the research argument, of course, is to find that the property's not eligible for the Register at all. "Come on," people beg the SHPO, "they're only a run-of-the-mill old barn and a lousy little scatter of stone flakes; you've got a million of each in the state. It's not eligible, is it? The governor doesn't think so." Of course, when a property's determined ineligible, this deprives it not only of the protections of Section 4(f) but also those of Section 106 as well. Not only does it not get protected in the absence of a feasible and prudent alternative, it doesn't even get considered in planning. That barn might very well not be something that anybody wants to keep on its present site in perpetuity, but it might be something worth moving and reusing someplace else, or at least documenting before it comes down. The flake scatter might not be much by itself, but its study, put together with the study of many other sites, might tell us something important about the past. If the barn is determined ineligible, it's unlikely that relocation or recordation will be done; if the flake scatter is found ineligible, the information it contains is probably going to go under the bulldozer without any effort to record it. And any other historic values either has—its importance to a farm family or a descendant community, for example—are going to be lost, too.

This sort of thing does not maintain the "integrity of historic preservation reviews," as the Trust's call to arms seems to suggest; it does quite the opposite. Absolute prohibitions, I think, corrupt planning. In making it impossible to do some things that are seen as bad, they tie the hands of planners in trying to do things that are good. They should be used, I think, very sparingly. I think that in writing Section 4(f), Congress meant to use its prohibitions sparingly, and I think we ought to try to get back to original intent.

Is there a way to do this without excising historic properties from Section 4(f) altogether? Probably. If one extended 4(f)'s prohibitions only to the use of historic properties that met certain standards above and beyond Register eligibility, I think one would come closer to what Congress had in mind and closer to balance with the consideration given parks and wildlife refuges. What might the standards be? Investment would certainly be one. Has someone—public or private—invested something of value in the property's preservation? Is it a locally designated historic district? Is it a house museum? Is it an interpreted archeological site? But because there are historic properties out there that are very important but in which nobody has yet happened to invest, it might be appropriate to go a bit further. One could define particular types of properties that would be given 4(f) protection. Indian spiritual sites, perhaps, or properties important to low-income populations and minority communities, to extend the logic of Executive Orders 13007 and 12898. Or National Historic Landmarks, though I think that would be foolish; many NHLs are important to experts (sometimes self-defined) at the National Park Service but to virtually nobody else. Or one could use a controversy standard—if people are really, really mad about the possibility that the Old Brown Barn will get torn down, maybe the Old Brown Barn should be given every reasonable opportunity to survive. Or perhaps one could use the Section 106 process—say that when the parties consulting under Section 106[3] can't reach agreement on how to resolve the adverse effects of a transportation project on historic properties, then Section 4(f) kicks in. I don't know exactly what the standard should be, but I think it's worth discussing. And I don't think it would be irresponsible for the historic preservation community to entertain such considerations. One might even see it as a mark of maturity.

Notes

1. Section 303 of the Act as amended and codified (49 U.S.C. 303) but still referred to by just about everyone as Section 4(f).

2. There are four National Register criteria, listed at 36 CFR 60.4. Criterion a is association with significant events or patterns of events in the past; Criterion b is association with significant people; Criterion c is met if a property exemplifies a type, style, period, or school of design, or meets one of several other subcriteria. Criterion d is met if a property has produced or may produce information important in history or prehistory.

3. Assuming good, comprehensive, fair, and fully informed consultation, not just deal-cutting between an agency and an SHPO.

11

The Letter of the Law

In the Section 106 classes I teach for the National Preservation Institute (NPI), we spend a good deal of time on how to initiate the review process—since a simple failure to do so is a common problem. The first two steps in getting the process started, under the regulations (36 CFR 800.3(a), to be exact), involve establishing whether a proposed action is an "undertaking" as defined in the statute—that is, whether it's under the direct or indirect authority of a federal agency—and whether it's the kind of action that has the potential to affect historic properties. In class we discuss kinds of actions that always have such potential—new construction, for example, and property transfers. We then discuss types of undertakings that don't realistically have such potential—hiring and firing personnel, buying office supplies, driving a government vehicle down the road. Then we turn to the gray zone—types of action that do, arguably at least, have the potential to affect historic properties but aren't subjected to 106 review and probably never will be.

One of my gray zone examples is the mortgage loan guarantee program of the Department of Veterans Affairs (DVA). I'm a veteran, and I bought my somewhat elderly home, in a somewhat antique neighborhood, with a DVA loan guarantee. The guarantee, having been issued by a federal agency, is obviously a federal undertaking. My home, or my neighborhood, might well be eligible for the National Register; I don't know, it's never been evaluated. I am something of a home handyman, but not a particularly skillful one. I know enough about the Secretary of the Interior's Standards for Rehabilitation to know that I've violated them in putting in my home office, adding a deck, changing some windows, and converting the garage to a family room. So facilitating my acquisition of this house was clearly something that had the potential to affect a historic property. Ergo, it should have been subjected to Section 106 review.

However, DVA loan guarantees (and similar guarantees by the Department of Housing and Urban Development) are never reviewed under Section 106, and it's very unlikely that they ever will be; a lawsuit seeking to force DVA or HUD to follow the Section 106 process every time it considered guaranteeing a loan would be laughed out of court. In class recently, a DVA attorney pointed out that there's an elementary rule of statutory construction that says you don't assume that Congress is nuts—you don't interpret a law to require agencies to do impossible things unless the statute specifically directs them to do so.

Fair enough, but upon reflection it occurred to me that the DVA lawyer and I were both making an incorrect assumption. We were both assuming that the law requires agencies to follow the standard Section 106 process set forth in the ACHP's regulations.

It would clearly be impossible—well, at least massively impractical—for DVA or HUD to go through the standard Section 106 process on every loan guarantee. In my case they would have had to (or required my bank or me to) determine whether my house and neighborhood were eligible for the National Register, in consultation with the SHPO and others. If either was eligible, they would have had to have negotiated a way either to keep me from having adverse effects, or to resolve the adverse effects I would have—or, of course, get and consider the ACHP's comments, or deny me the guarantee. They couldn't realistically do any of these things without greatly distorting their loan guarantee programs, particularly considering the volume of transactions they process each year (which must, I suppose, run into the hundreds of thousands).

But the statute itself—NHPA at Section 106—doesn't require an agency to do all that stuff; it simply requires them to take effects on historic properties into account and afford the ACHP a reasonable opportunity to comment. Section 110(a)(2)(E) also requires each agency to have Section 106 compliance procedures that provide for identification and evaluation of properties, consultation, and agreements, but it doesn't say at what level of abstraction these things have to take place.

So if we go back to the letter of the law, for a moment ignoring the regulations, would it be possible for DVA or HUD to comply with Section 106 on loan guarantee cases? Of course it would.

For example, they could acknowledge the likelihood that some percentage of their loan guarantees would permit butterfingered home carpenters like me to acquire historic buildings in historic districts and work their wills on them. They could then ask themselves, and their consulting partners, what they could do to resolve the adverse effects that people like me would visit upon such properties—with the understanding that there's nothing in the law that says they can't allow such effects, nor that they have to mitigate them in any particular way. The only semi-substantive direction given by the statute is at Section 2(4), where agencies are directed to "contribute to the preservation of nonfederally owned prehistoric and historic resources."

So how, within the scopes of their missions and what they can reasonably ask Congress to appropriate, could DVA and HUD "take into account" the effects of loan guarantees on historic properties in a manner that contributes to the preservation of such resources? There are probably several possibilities, but the one that comes to my mind is simply to use the loan guarantee process as an educational opportunity. Put together a simple little brochure about why and how to take good care of an old house in an old neighborhood, and make the brochure easily available to every applicant for and recipient of a loan guarantee, probably through banks and mortgage companies. DVA and HUD would thus provide guidance—nothing required, but encouragement to do right—to a targeted audience of people who own and control buildings, numbering in the hundreds of thousands if not millions.

Would such a thing guarantee that all historic buildings purchased using DVA or HUD loan guarantees are maintained in accordance with the Secretary's Standards? No, but it would certainly increase the likelihood that a lot of such buildings—and as the information diffused through the loan-making and home ownership networks, a lot of buildings purchased *without* such guarantees as well—would be maintained with some degree of sensitivity for their architectural qualities. It might well have a far more

positive overall effect on the preservation of historic buildings and neighborhoods than would imposition of the standard Section 106 process—
even if such imposition were technically, economically, and politically feasible.

As for meeting legal requirements, since distribution of the guidance
would (hopefully) contribute to the preservation of nonfederally owned
historic (and prehistoric, if guidance about being careful when digging
were included) resources, the agencies would be in compliance with Section 2(4). By recognizing the need for such an information campaign the
agencies would have taken the effects of their actions into account in accordance with Section 106. I don't think it would tax a clever lawyer too
much to find that the specific identification and evaluation requirements
of Section 110(a)(2)(E) wouldn't need to be adhered to in this case, provided the overall DVA and HUD programs provided for them to be met
where specific agency effects on specific properties were anticipated. By
consulting with SHPOs, THPOs, the ACHP, and other interested parties
in developing the educational program, the agencies would arguably be in
compliance with the requirement of the same subsection to consult and
implement agreements about the consideration of adverse effects. Such
consultation with the ACHP would also satisfy the requirement of Section 106 that the ACHP be given a "reasonable opportunity to comment."
The last pertinent legal requirement, subsection 110(a)(2)(E)(i), which requires agency Section 106 programs to be consistent with regulations issued by the ACHP, would be satisfied if the educational program were
embodied in a Programmatic Agreement or another of the "program alternatives" offered by the regulations at 36 CFR 800.14.

Enough statutory and regulatory citations. And enough picking on
DVA and HUD, which may or may not ever go to the trouble of bringing
their loan guarantee programs into compliance with Section 106; they're
not under any pressure to do so. My main point is simply that when we
think about whether a given agency program, or project for that matter,
can practically be brought into compliance with Section 106 when there
are impediments to doing so, we need to avoid focusing narrowly on the
specific requirements of the standard regulatory process. We need to go
back to the letter of the law and figure out how, practically speaking, in the
real world, the agency can do what Congress told it to do. Once we've fig-

ured this out, the regulations provide a host of ways to document that what has been agreed upon constitutes compliance with Section 106.

The other reason I've included this chapter is that I think the solution outlined above to DVA's and HUD's (perhaps unperceived) problem is one that could apply in a number of other situations where agencies provide diffuse advice and assistance to private parties. Technical assistance provided by the Farm Services Agency and the Natural Resources Conservation Service in the Department of Agriculture comes to mind as an example, along with several assistance and partnership programs of the Fish and Wildlife Service. We might get a lot more bang for such agencies' compliance bucks by using their advice, assistance, and cooperative programs as educational vehicles than by trying to impose upon them a detailed system of project-by-project review that was designed with things like highways, reservoirs, and urban renewal projects in mind.

12

*Guidance from a Good SHPO**

I recently had occasion to review some instructions to agencies, put out by an SHPO who will remain nameless. The guidance detailed the kinds of documents the SHPO expected to be submitted to it in compliance with the Section 106 regulations. It was a pretty depressing little item—well, not so little, about twenty pages—bearing scant relationship to the actual requirements of the regulations. Sometimes, in fact, it stood these requirements on their heads, for example by requiring all kinds of detailed survey work before identifying and talking with concerned parties, or without bothering to do so at all. It created the strong impression that what Section 106 is all about is submitting massive paperwork to the SHPO and getting sign-off. It was clearly the work of what my own SHPO, Rodney Little of Maryland, used to call a "PDS"—petty dictatorial SHPO—and one with a passionate penchant for paperwork.

Unfortunately, what I saw was not an isolated case, though it was extreme. SHPOs across the country are generating similar "requirements" that they lay on hapless project proponents who seek their assistance with Section 106 review.

When I asked an Advisory Council staff member about the guidelines I'd seen, and their inaccurate portrayal of the Section 106 process, the reaction I got was, in effect: "Well, if these SHPO instructions are so bad,

---

*Modified somewhat from an original Internet note posted on ACRA-L, 1999.

we'll be happy to consider doing something *positive* about them, but we don't want to criticize."

Seems like a helluva way to exercise the oversight the Council says it's supposed to exercise in lieu of participating in case-by-case review, but so be it; I tried to think positively. What, I thought, would be useful and appropriate for an SHPO to put out to its Section 106 consulting partners in the way of guidance about documentation under the regulations? I turned for advice to my old friend, the Washafornia SHPO, and she sent me the following to share with people to use, adapt, or recommend to others as they see fit.

Letter Sent by Washafornia SHPO to All Agencies, Local Governments, Consulting Firms, and Others That Undertake Section 106 Review of Projects

Dear Colleagues,

As you know, in 1999 and again in 2000, the Advisory Council on Historic Preservation (ACHP) revised its regulations (36 CFR 800) for implementing Section 106 of the National Historic Preservation Act. These revisions affect how we all do our Section 106 business. I thought it would be helpful for me to spell out the kind of documentation we would like you to provide us at each step in the Section 106 process, in order to facilitate our review under the regulations.

Before we turn to documentation, though, I want to draw your attention to Section 800.8 of the regulations, on coordination with the National Environmental Policy Act (NEPA). Section 800.8(a)(3) stresses the need to be sure that historic preservation issues are addressed in NEPA analyses, and Section 800.8(b) gives special attention to NEPA categorical exclusions, while Section 800.8(c) provides for the use of NEPA analyses and documents to satisfy Section 106 requirements. We would be very happy to work with you to review your procedures for NEPA compliance in order to ensure that preservation issues are considered, particularly on projects that are categorically excluded from detailed NEPA analysis. We would also like to learn more about your NEPA procedures so that we can interact with you better. Please feel free to contact me at your convenience to discuss this.

Turning now to documentation:

1. At Section 800.3 the regulations deal extensively with how to initiate Section 106 review. This is a very important topic; often the inadvertent failure to initiate the process early enough, or to think through what's needed to get the process underway, causes serious complications as review proceeds (*if* it proceeds).

Initiating the 106 process first involves deciding whether the proposed action is an undertaking, and whether it requires review. Virtually everything a federal agency does, or assists, or permits, or oversees is an undertaking, but an undertaking is subject to review only if it is the type of action that has the potential to affect historic properties. This means that personnel actions, purchase of office supplies, and routine vehicle movements, for example, don't require review, but anything that may affect buildings or land does. It is important to recognize that you do *not* have to know (or even suspect) that historic properties may be affected; if the action is the *type* of thing that *can* affect historic properties, it requires review. Note, too, that *all* kinds of effects need to be considered—direct, indirect, and cumulative (See Section 800.5(a)(1)). In marginal or questionable cases, we will be happy to help you figure out whether your undertaking requires review.

In initiating review the regulations also call for coordinating with other reviews, such as NEPA and the Native American Graves Protection and Repatriation Act (NAGPRA). You are also to figure out which SHPO(s) or Tribal Historic Preservation Officer(s) (THPOs) you need to deal with, plan to involve the public, and identify consulting parties *besides* the SHPO or THPO, so they can be effectively involved in the process.

The regulations allow for combining multiple steps in the process, provided this doesn't deprive the consulting parties and the public of their opportunity to understand what's going on and to participate. We anticipate that many agencies will want to combine starting review with scoping for identification of historic properties (Section 800.4). Scoping involves defining the area(s) of potential effect (APE), reviewing background data, seeking new data from consulting parties, and identifying issues that may need to be addressed. The purpose of scoping, as the name implies, is to establish the scope of work for identification—what sorts of properties will be sought, what kinds of methods will be used, what kinds of personnel will be required, and so on.

The regulations do not tell us what kind of documentation should be put together when initiating review, or for scoping, but in order to meet the requirements summarized above, we suggest that when you first con-tact our office about a project, you answer as many of the following ques-tions as you can, with whatever supporting documentation is available. You should be prepared to share all this with other consulting parties as well:

Documentation for Initiating Review and Scoping

1. What is the undertaking? What is the purpose of or need for it?

2. What alternatives are you considering for carrying it out?

3. What do you think its APE is, and why? Remember that all kinds of effects must be considered—direct, indirect, cumulative. Please provide a map or maps if possible.

4. Who besides this office do you think you need to consult about the undertaking and its effects on historic properties? Do you need any help finding potential consulting parties?

5. How are you planning to involve the public? The regulations encourage use of NEPA public participation activities to satisfy Sec-tion 106 review requirements, but these procedures must give the public an adequate basis for understanding historic preservation issues and the review process, and an appropriate opportunity to actually participate in consultation (36 CFR 800.2(d)(3)).

6. How are you handling this undertaking under NEPA? Is it likely to be categorically excluded, or will you do an Environmental Assess-ment (EA) or Environmental Impact Statement (EIS)?

7. Are there other cultural resource laws or related requirements you think you need to address—for example, NAGPRA, or the Arche-ological and Historic Preservation Act, or Executive Order 12898 on Environmental Justice with respect to cultural environmental matters?

8. What do you think you need to do to identify historic properties? This can take the form of a draft scope of work. Note that for large areas, corridors, and situations where access is limited, a "phased" approach may be appropriate, in which historic property types and

areas of sensitivity are predicted at an early phase, with provisions for testing predictions at later phases (36 CFR 800.4(b)(2)). If you want to pursue this kind of approach, please be as specific as you can about proposed work to be done at each phase, and how you propose to coordinate identification phases with 106 review, NEPA, and overall project planning.

9. How do you plan to document the results of identification? Are there confidentiality issues, or other reasons to limit the scope of documentation? Are there particular forms or formats for documentation that you propose to use?

10. How would you like our office to be involved? Please understand that our staff and time are limited, and that we are not responsible for doing the work that's assigned to you by the regulations, but with these caveats we will be happy to help in any way we can.

Please try to provide the above information in a clear and organized form that's easy for us to assimilate. If you can, organize it into the form of a work plan made up of specific proposals with justifications, so we can efficiently document our concurrence, questions, or objections. If you organize the material in this way and do not get a response from us within thirty (30) days after we receive the material, you can assume our concurrence in your work plan. However, please note that a request from us for more information, if sent to you within this thirty-day period and including a reasonable rationale for our request, constitutes a response, and the thirty-day clock doesn't start ticking again until you have provided us with the information we requested or explained why you can't supply it.

If you provide the above information to us (and to other consulting parties) when you initiate review, it should be relatively easy for us to work with you to finalize plans for identification, including appropriate scopes of work, and to coordinate with you as identification proceeds.

Documentation for Consensus Determinations of Eligibility/Ineligibility

The purpose of identification under Section 106 is to find historic properties—or to predict historic property types—that may be eligible for inclusion in the National Register of Historic Places, and to determine what effects may occur to them. You need to document identified properties well enough to permit you to reach grounded conclusions about their eligibility and about effects on them, and for us and others to consider and comment on your opinions. Issues to be addressed in determining and resolving adverse effects should also be identified where possible, and people and groups to be consulted about historic properties and effects should be sought.

In conducting identification, please be sure to consider the full range of property types that may exist and may be subject to direct, indirect, or cumulative effects. These often include, for example, cultural landscapes, traditional cultural properties, and linear features like roads and trails, as well as buildings, structures, and archeological sites. It is not necessary to identify *all* historic properties subject to effect. What is required is a reasonable and good faith effort to identify historic properties in enough detail to permit defensible decisions to be made about effects. Particularly where indirect effects are involved, far less than "complete" identification may be appropriate. We will be happy to discuss with you what may be an appropriately "reasonable" level and kind of identification.

Please also remember that cultural resources *other than* historic properties may be affected by your undertaking—for example, traditional ways of life, historical documents, sources of historical, archeological, and scientific data that aren't eligible for the National Register, and Native American cultural items in sites that aren't eligible for the Register. We will be happy to consult with you about how to address such resources, but please understand that our formal consultative responsibilities extend only to the requirements of Section 106. Other resources will need to be considered under NEPA, NAGPRA, and other authorities.

36 CFR 800.4(c)(2) deals with determining eligibility/ineligibility for the National Register. No documentation requirements are specified. We suggest that during scoping, you discuss with us how such determinations should be documented. Note that you are *not* required to prepare National Register nomination forms on properties you think may be eligible (or ineligible). We like to receive a completed Form WASH238NiTPiK on each possible historic property identified, but we understand that it is not always feasible, cost-effective, or appropriate to provide this level of detail. Please discuss with us what level

of detail *should* be developed, *before* you finalize a scope of work for identification.

Generally speaking, we anticipate that data on possible historic properties will be presented in a written report, in sufficient detail to allow us to understand:

1. Approximately where each property is (precise boundaries need be specified only where relevant to determining effects);

2. What each property is; and

3. Why you do or do not think it is eligible for the National Register.

Where it is not possible to document each of the items above (for example, where tribal concerns preclude revealing property locations and other characteristics), please explain why the documentation cannot be provided. We would appreciate being consulted in advance if it appears that some bodies of information will have to be kept from us.

If you have not identified specific properties, but predicted locations of property types (as you might in a phased identification effort, for example), you should document what types of properties are predicted, where they are likely to be, and why you do or do not think each predicted type is likely to be eligible.

You should also document the methods employed in background research, consultation, and fieldwork, and who you've consulted in reaching your conclusions.

Documentation for "No Historic Properties Subject to Effect" Findings

If your identification results in the conclusion either that there just aren't any historic properties in the APE, or that there are (or may be) such properties but they won't be affected by the undertaking, then 36 CFR 800.4(d) provides for determining that there are "no historic properties subject to effect." With such a determination, you must provide specific documentation to our office and to other consulting parties, and allow 30 days for our review and response. Section 800.11(d) lays out the documentation requirements, summarized below with our suggestions:

1. Description of the undertaking and the APE. If you have already submitted this information you don't have to do so again; just refer to it and describe any changes that have occurred since you submitted it in the first place.

2. Description of the steps taken to identify historic properties. This will normally be a summary of work done under the scope of work developed during scoping; if we participated in development of the scope, you can simply refer to the scope we assisted you in developing, but you may have to provide more detail for consulting parties who were *not* involved in the scoping and identification processes.

3. The basis for determining that no historic properties are present or affected. Outline the rationale for your conclusion. If there are uncertainties—for example, the possibility that historic properties were missed for some reason, or if untested predictions have been used with respect to areas of indirect impact, these should be explained and proposals offered for dealing with them. In some cases a Memorandum of Agreement including a system for handling discoveries may be appropriate. Where phased identification is used, your finding at this point may be conditioned upon future work (e.g., "Studies to date suggest that there are no historic properties in the APE of Alternative C because they were all washed out in the flood of 1976, but if this alternative becomes the preferred alternative, the following will be done to confirm or disconfirm this prediction.").

Finding of No Adverse Effect or Adverse Effect

If historic properties *will* be affected, then in consultation with this office and other consulting parties, you apply the Criteria of Adverse Effect (Sec. 800.5(a)(1)). If you find that there's no adverse effect you document this finding and, if we don't object within 30 days, you can proceed. If you find that there *is* an adverse effect, or if we *do* object, then we go on to consult further about resolving the adversity. Either way, you provide all the consulting parties with the documentation summarized and discussed below (based on Sec. 800.11(e):

1. Description of the undertaking, etc. Again, you don't need to supply this if we already have it, but you need to be sure that all the consulting parties have it.

2. Description of the steps taken to identify historic properties. If we already have this (e.g., a survey report), we don't need it again. But as above, make sure that all the consulting parties have it unless you (or the responsible federal agency, if you're not such an agency) have determined, in consultation with the Keeper of the National Register under Section 304 of the NHPA, that some or all of the information must be held confidential.

3. Description of the affected historic properties, including the qualities that make them eligible for the National Register. As with the preceding items, if we already have this information you need not provide it again, but subject to NHPA Section 304 you should be sure the other consulting parties have it. In some cases—notably when identification and effect determination are "phased," we understand that this description may be rather generic (for example: "The association of Southeast Garveytown with the development of the popcorn industry, and the fact that its buildings exemplify West Washafornia vernacular warehouse architecture, leads us to conclude that this neighborhood constitutes an eligible historic district.").

4. A description of the undertaking's effects on historic properties. This should be keyed to the list of "examples" given at Sec. 800.5(a)(2) if possible. Here again the description can be generic if appropriate (for example: "Having predicted that Southeast Garveytown may constitute a historic district, we can also predict that expanding the Pink Cadillac Parkway along its eastern periphery may cause traffic congestion that will introduce incompatible visual and auditory elements into the district.").

5. An explanation of why the criteria of adverse effect were found applicable or inapplicable. We do not interpret this to mean that you must demonstrate how each and every effect of the action does or does not meet the overall criterion set forth in Section 800.5(a)(1) (altering the characteristics of a property that contribute to its eligibility, in a way that diminishes its integrity). Nor do we think it means you have to go through each of the examples set forth in Section 800.5(a)(2) and discuss how it does and does not apply. A simple narrative about how you think the effects of the action relate to the criteria will be sufficient—for example: "The action's predicted effects do not meet the Criteria of Adverse Effect set forth at 36 CFR 800.5(a)(1) and (2), except that the destruction of the Meagerquartz Flake Scatter Site will

obviously destroy the integrity of this property and hence is an adverse effect."

6. Anything you propose to do to avoid, minimize, or mitigate adverse effects. In the case of a "no adverse effect" finding, such proposed actions must be sufficient to actually avoid, or eliminate, any realistic projected adverse effect. In the case of an "adverse effect" finding, you can propose measures that reduce or compensate for the effect, or even propose to accept the effect in the public interest without mitigation. For example, you can propose to design a project to completely avoid an archeological site as a condition of a "no adverse effect" determination, but excavating the site before destroying it can be proposed only as mitigation based on an "adverse effect" finding. Where identification, evaluation, and effect determination are "phased," the measures proposed may also be laid out in phases—for example: "If Alternative 5A appears to be the preferred alternative overall, we will conduct further traffic studies to define the severity of traffic impacts on the district in greater detail, and work with the SHPO, the Southeast Garveytown neighborhood commission, and other consulting parties to find ways of mitigating such impacts. At least the following mechanisms will be considered."

7. Copies or summaries of the views of consulting parties and the public. Although we will probably have copies of these views, it is usually a good idea to organize and submit them at this point, in order to make sure that no one's ideas have gotten lost along the way.

Substituting NEPA Analysis and Documents

Section 800.8(c) permits you to substitute the conduct and review of NEPA analyses and documents for standard Section 106 review, provided certain conditions are met, and provided you notify this office and the ACHP that you intend to do so. If you are interested in such substitution, I urge you to contact us to discuss the possibility, and to notify us early in planning—either programmatically or on a case-by-case basis—so we can work with you to explore creative ways to make NEPA and Section 106 work together.

Delegation to Applicants

Section 800.2(c)(5) permits agencies to delegate the "legwork" of initiating Section 106 review to applicants for assistance and permits. The agency remains responsible for the quality of its Section 106 compliance, however (Sec. 800.2(a)(3)). If you plan to delegate such work, the regulations require you to notify this office in advance. If you will routinely delegate, we suggest that you notify us programmatically.

General Documentation Standard

The general documentation standard set forth in Section 800.11(a) is that the agency "shall ensure that a determination, finding, or agreement . . . is supported by sufficient documentation to enable any reviewing parties to understand its basis." Please take this standard to heart in interpreting all the specific recommendations above. The documentation you provide us should, *please,* be organized in a way that makes it easy for us to understand what you are saying, and to respond to you in an efficient way.

Please feel free to contact me or any of my colleagues in this office to discuss these recommendations and the requirements of the regulations. We look forward to working with you in the future.

13

A Consultant's Duty

The other day I had a call from a client—the representative of a CRM subcontractor to an environmental impact assessment subcontractor to an engineering firm whose contract was with our ultimate client, the proponent of a sizeable civil works project. The subject of the call isn't important; what stuck with me is an offhand remark that my caller made in passing. It went something like this:

"We certainly hope that this project goes forward in some form or other and that we can continue to be a part of it."

An understandable sentiment, surely; my caller and my fellow consultants up and down the contract food chain are all making their living in substantial part by working on the project; if it were to go away, we would all be the poorer. But the statement still bothered me, and continues to.

Part of the reason it bothers me is that a while before our conversation, I'd seen a printout of an e-mail exchange (obtained via a Freedom of Information Act request) among CRM specialists representing a federal agency involved in the same project, evaluating the claims and counterclaims of project opponents and proponents. The correspondents dismissed one of my documents (a masterpiece of objective analysis, in my view) because:

"King is, of course, paid to tell the (proponents) what they want to hear."

In point of fact—as I, at least, understand the facts, and as the ultimate client in this case has assured me it understands them—I am by no means paid to tell anybody what they want to hear, nor to advance the ultimate client's interests. My job is to give the client objective advice about the subjects that fall within my area of expertise. This job includes analysis and critique of the statements and representations of project opponents, some of which I have found to be pretty exotic and have said so. But my job is also to tell the proponents when I think they're wrong, and suggest ways to make their approaches more consistent with law, regulation, and good practice as I understand it. Which I've done with some enthusiasm. And when I'm asked to analyze something and write a report, it's supposed to be an objective report, not one designed to support my client's (or anyone else's) point of view.

But it is not the point of this essay to explain my relationship to my client. My concern about the two statements quoted above is that they seem to reflect the shared, and uncritically accepted, notion that a consultant's job is to advance the interests of his or her client. I think this is a very dangerous proposition.

My telephone caller apparently took it for granted that he should want the project to proceed—after all, it's his bread and butter. And he took it for granted that I should feel the same way, presumably for the same reason. The Internet reviewer made the same assumption, thus justifying himself in rejecting my analysis out of hand, without serious consideration.

Is this what everyone assumes? If so, how can any consultant ever be credible?

Searching my own heart after my disturbing phone conversation, I thought, and think, that I can honestly say that I don't give a damn whether the project in question goes forward, in any form at all. Moreover, I think I would regard it as seriously damaging to my credibility if I *did* want the project to proceed, and I think I'd be doing my client a disservice if I had such a desire. My job is to give objective advice and analysis, period.

What, then, do I owe my client? Exclusive access to and possession of my advice and the results of my analyses, except where the client directs or authorizes me to share them with somebody else. A good example arose some years ago when a project proponent asked me to review documentation on an area that was claimed to be a Native American spiritual site eligible for inclusion in the National Register of Historic Places as a "traditional cultural property." My job was to analyze its probable eligibility. My client didn't want it to be eligible because it stood in the way of his project. My conclusion was that it was as eligible as the day is long. I so advised my client and no one else; the client took my conclusion and, I suppose, burned it, but backed off from opposing the site's eligibility.

I would have been violating my obligation to the client had I shared my analysis with project opponents, or the State Historic Preservation Officer, or anybody else without the client's authorization. But I would equally be violating my obligation to the client if I "told him what he wanted to hear."

But what about cases where I really *do* support the project? Or more often, really do oppose it? In a recent case on the west coast, my client was a tribe that vehemently opposed a surface mine in an area of cultural and religious importance. I agreed entirely with the tribe and wrote comments accordingly on environmental documents and representations by the project's proponents. I really did (and do) want the project *not* to go forward. What's my obligation in such a case?

To my client, I again clearly owe objective advice. I can't tell the client that the law says something it doesn't say, or that the client's case is stronger (or weaker) than it is. I owe the same objectivity to outside reviewers. If I assert something about, say, the potential impacts of the project, I need to articulate an argument supporting my opinion that's grounded in fact and/ or in law. And I need to be very, very careful about letting my values bias my judgment.

I recently read a report that purported to identify traditional cultural properties in a project's impact area. It ended with words along the following lines:

The tribe has a long history of association with this area; therefore, the devastating impacts of this project are real and should be taken very seriously.

Wait a minute. Given that the tribe has a long association with the area, what does that have to do with the "reality" of the project's impacts? The two clauses don't relate intelligibly to one another, but what the second clause *does* do is reveal the bias of the author. The author thinks (though as it happens, the report didn't show) that the project will have very damaging effects; the strong implication is that he doesn't want the project to be approved. What he said may or may not be what his client wanted to hear, but it certainly reflects an attitude that calls the objectivity of the analysis into question.

I think it's all right—and certainly sometimes unavoidable—to have opinions about whether a project we're consulting on should or should not go forward. But I think that at the very least we need to reveal our opinions, and think through, and try to control, the ways they may bias the way we carry out and report our work.

But I guess the thing that really bothers me about the telephone conversation that stimulated me to write this piece is the seemingly unquestioned assumption that a consultant should want his client's interests to be served *because the client is paying the consultant.* Not because the consultant believes the client's interests are the public's interests, or are consistent with law and good public policy, or will be beneficial or at least not too damaging to the environment, but simply because the client is paying the tab. I think this sort of attitude vitiates the whole enterprise of environmental consultation. We've got to be paid to live, but we shouldn't be bought. When it's tacitly assumed on all sides that by virtue of being hired we *have* been bought, then I think we've got a real problem.

Part III

Thinking about Indigenous Issues

Over the last five hundred plus years, the U.S. and state governments have displayed schizoid attitudes toward Indian tribes and other indigenous groups (e.g., Inuits, Polynesians, Micronesians). Official government policy toward tribes has oscillated wildly between assimilation and apartheid—in some decades isolating them on reservations, in others breaking up reservations and trying to absorb Indian individuals into the great American melting pot. Policy toward other indigenous groups has mostly been one of benign neglect, coupled with pious expressions of appreciation for their unique cultures.

Until the 1980s, when indigenous activism forced the mainstream to pay attention, CRM law and practice largely ignored native peoples and their concerns. Their ancestral homesites, cemeteries, and shrines were assumed to be the province of archeologists, and their living societies that of ethnographers. The notion that they themselves could be players in the CRM game was novel. Change came rapidly during the 1980s and 1990s, but there is still a great deal of uncertainty—among indigenous groups and institutional CRM alike—about the roles tribes and other native groups should play and the ways they should be treated. Should a Tribal Historic Preservation Officer (THPO) meet the same standards and follow the same guidelines as a State Historic Preservation Officer (SHPO)? If not, why not? Does it matter that the standards applied to the latter were developed with reference to cultural norms, and in a socioeconomic context, that may be foreign to the former? To what extent should the desires of indigenous groups about resources important to them determine how such resources are managed? How much should native interests influence federal decision making? How should one find out what those interests are? How should an indigenous group be expected to demonstrate its interests? To what extent, and how, should it be expected to prove its case? In what sociocultural, legal, and administrative contexts should disputes between indigenous groups and others be worked out? What should an agency or project proponent do to determine whether such disputes may exist? People think they know the answers to such questions, but the answers range all over the map.

In this environment of uncertainty, Congress has made laws, presidents have issued executive orders, agencies have issued regulations, and practitioners have evolved standards, guidelines, and ways of doing business. The most famous of the CRM-related laws is the Native American Graves Protection and Repatriation Act, which is the subject of the first chapter in this section. NAGPRA is widely and to some extent correctly regarded as a law that for better or worse gave tribes control over museums and their collections, as well as over archeologists. I suggest that it has had some other unintended consequences. The second chapter focuses on another well-known point of interaction between indigenous people and cultural resource managers—the identification and management of "traditional cultural properties." The third addresses a specific, always pesky aspect of CRM practice with respect to "TCPs"—that of permissible scale. Finally, the fourth chapter is about consultation between tribes and others (such as federal agencies), some standard CRM practices and assumptions that get in the way of effective consultation, and what might be done about them.

14

What's Really Wrong with NAGPRA

A great deal of vitriol has been spilled over NAGPRA—the Native American Graves Protection and Repatriation Act. Some archeologists and physical anthropologists (but by no means all, as some elements of the popular press would have us believe) hate NAGPRA and, more importantly, everything it stands for. They regard it as government sponsorship of religion, on a par with governmental bans on the teaching of evolution. They argue that the human remains and cultural items to which NAGPRA applies should be preserved and studied to enrich all humankind, rather than given to particular Indian tribes—who may do with them as they please and may not have "legitimate" rights to the things anyhow. Tribes tend to support NAGPRA as a very partial redress of grievances visited upon them by whites, as a token of respect to the ancestors, as a way of putting sacred objects and ancestral remains back where they belong, and as a way of healing old wounds. Increasingly, though, tribes and their members are becoming concerned about the conflicts—including intertribal conflicts—that NAGPRA engenders and about its mind-numbingly legalistic character.

I'm an archeologist, and I don't like NAGPRA much, but not for the reasons that most displeased archeologists cite. I think NAGPRA does damage to the cultural and spiritual integrity, and the sovereignty, of tribes.

NAGPRA was designed to address a very real set of problems—that the ancestors of Indian tribes aren't given the same respect as everybody else's ancestors; that the remains of such ancestors, and their treasured cultural items, have in many cases been taken from tribes without authority to do so; that ancestral remains and cultural items have lain for decades in museums and storerooms, sometimes even been discarded, without the permission or even the knowledge of descendants. In testimony before Congress in the late 1980s, tribal representatives spoke eloquently of the cultural wrongs done them by the majority society—sometimes quite ghastly wrongs. They impressed the members of Congress enough to gain enactment of NAGPRA—a piece of legislation worked out through negotiation among tribes, Native Hawaiian groups, archeologists, physical anthropologists, and museum officials. Or rather, worked out by their lawyers, and therein, I think, lies NAGPRA's real problem. NAGPRA is a classic example of why the design of laws should never be left entirely to lawyers.

NAGPRA is grounded in property law. It declares ancestral remains and "Native American cultural items"—funerary objects, sacred objects, and "objects of cultural patrimony"—to be the property of lineal descendants and culturally affiliated tribes and Native Hawaiian groups. It then directs federal agencies and federally assisted museums to repatriate such remains and items to the tribes and groups that own them. The procedures for repatriation are quite complicated, largely because of the need to determine just who really is a lineal descendant or culturally affiliated group.

The "scientific" objections to NAGPRA spring from the perception that "archeological resources" and the information they contain belong to all humanity. In other words, these objections too are grounded in property law—in who owns what.

But how does the notion of ancestral remains and cultural items as property relate to tribal values and beliefs?

Let's back up a moment and ask ourselves why tribes want repatriation of ancestral remains and cultural items. In point of fact I'm not sure they always do, particularly where ancestral remains are concerned. Typically in my experience, repatriation itself isn't the goal; it's a means to an end. The desired end is to get the remains back into the ground, where they can return to the soil as the ancestors they represent continue their journey to the spirit world. This "back to the earth" philosophy is not universal, and there are lots of variations on the theme. I don't think there's any tribe, however, that wants its ancestors back in order to possess them.

Generally speaking, the same rationale motivates the desire to "get back" funerary items—it's not that the tribes want them for themselves; they want them to accompany the ancestors into—and in many beliefs beyond—the grave. With sacred items and objects of cultural patrimony it's a little different—sacred objects by definition are needed for the conduct of ceremonies, and objects of cultural patrimony—well, the definition of such objects is so strange and circumloquacious that it might mean almost anything. But the central things that NAGPRA is about—ancestral remains and grave goods—are usually not wanted back to possess as property but to return to the ground where their spiritual qualities can be properly respected and the reasons for which they were buried in the first place can be realized. Thus there's at best an uncertain fit between the rationale for repatriation and the tools—identification and return to qualified "owners"—that NAGPRA provides to implement that rationale. I believe that this conflict undercuts and erodes the whole purpose of NAGPRA.

In the mid-1980s I was at the Advisory Council on Historic Preservation, and one of my jobs was to work with the Indian tribes and intertribal groups that were getting more and more involved in Section 106 review. One of the organizations I dealt with a good deal was American Indians Against Desecration (AIAD), a branch of the American Indian Movement (AIM). AIAD essentially consisted of Jan Hammil and a group of advising elders from various tribes. Jan, herself of Comanche extraction, made her living as a judge on the night court in Indianapolis, giving her the daylight hours free to work for AIAD. I have no idea when she slept; she may not have needed to. Jan was one of the most dynamic people I've ever met, and she never shrank from confrontation. Her—and AIAD's—mission was to get the remains of the ancestors back into the ground, and she did everything she could to carry out that mission. One of those things being to jawbone the Advisory Council—i.e., me—about what we should be doing to support reburial. Not repatriation, note; reburial.

One day I was talking with Jan, and offered up the (then) usual "moderate" archeological line:

"If it's somebody's grandmother, of course she should be given back to the descendants for reburial, but if it's somebody ancient . . ."

"Look, dummy," Jan said kindly (or words to that effect), "this has nothing to do with ownership, or exactly who's descended from whom. I don't own my grandmother's bones. Nobody can own another person; the Civil War established that."

"Yeah, but . . ."

"It's about respect," she said. "Respect for ancestors—everybody's ancestors. I respect your ancestors, my ancestors, even (the Interior Departmental Consulting Archeologist's) ancestors, and the way to respect them is by taking care of them, trying to make sure that they can continue their journey to the spirit world."

It was an epiphany for me. It so simplified things. If it's all about respect, not ownership, then we don't need to worry about the complicated business of deciding who's descended from which skeleton in the ground. We don't have to argue about whether a 10,000-year-old dead guy has any living relatives, or whether he represents an ancestor of the group that occupied the land in 1870 or some other group. And we don't necessarily have to put everything back in the ground. We don't see an autopsy as disrespectful, nor the forensic analysis of possible crime victims. In the same way, there might be ways to analyze ancient human remains respectfully; perhaps even keep some of them out of the ground in perpetuity. In any event, if consultation between archeologists, agencies, and tribes focused on how to treat ancestors respectfully, rather than on ownership, we'd at least be consulting about something on which an agreement *might* be reached.

We tried to use this notion of respect as the groundwork for treating human remains and associated artifacts; the Advisory Council even established a policy statement based on such principles[1] to guide consulting parties in Section 106 review. The core of the statement went like this:

- Human remains and grave goods should not be disinterred unless required in advance of some kind of disturbance, such as construction.

- Disinterment when necessary should be done carefully, respect-fully, and completely, in accordance with proper archeological methods.

- In general, human remains and grave goods should be reburied, in consultation with the descendants of the dead.

- Prior to reburial, scientific studies should be performed as nec-essary to address justified research topics.

- Scientific studies and reburial should occur according to a def-inite, agreed-upon schedule.

- Where scientific study is offensive to the descendants of the dead, and the need for such study does not outweigh the need to respect the concerns of such descendants, reburial should oc-cur without prior study. Conversely, where the scientific re-search value of human remains and grave goods outweighs any objections that descendants may have to their study, they should not be reburied, but should be retained in perpetuity for study.

OK, so like NAGPRA, the policy statement referred a good deal to "descendants," but it demanded respect for the dead, and generally rebur-ial, whether there were descendants or not. And since we weren't talking about ownership but only participation in consultation, "descendants" could be defined broadly. In guidance issued to the Council's staff about how to interpret the policy statement, "descendants of the dead" was de-fined as:

Any group, community, or organization that may be related culturally or by descent to the deceased persons represented by human remains.[2]

Were either the tribes or the archeologists entirely thrilled with the Council's policy? No, but both seemed able to live with it, to try it out. Both, I think, at least saw it as balanced and respectful of both the dead and of the interests of the living. But then along came NAGPRA and threw it all into a cocked hat. Because NAGPRA took us back to the grandmother argument, and ignored respect altogether.

Of course, one thing that made the property-law basis for NAGPRA attractive to the lawyers who negotiated it was that it (theoretically) made possible hard-and-fast, clearly definable determinations. The bones or objects either did or did not actually belong to the agency or museum; they either did or did not belong to this tribe or that. All very desirable to those who insist that life and human relations be reduced to rules. But when one begins to apply the rules—even in the abstract as the drafters of the statute did during its negotiation—things begin to get very complicated. What makes sense in one situation does not in another. The result, in the case of NAGPRA, was a complicated layering of procedures for determining cultural affiliation and right of possession, with burdens of proof shifting back and forth between tribes and museums or agencies as the procedures are implemented.

Consider a couple of real-world examples:

At Chaco Canyon, the National Park Service has the unenviable task of repatriating human remains excavated over the years from the area's ancient pueblo ruins. But to whom should they be repatriated? The NPS has made what seems like a good-faith effort to figure out the answer. It concluded that while the Hopi and other puebloan groups in the area obviously have claims, so do the Navajo. After all, by the most conservative of reckonings the Navajo have been in the area for several centuries, and it would be strange indeed if there hadn't been some mingling of genes and culture. Besides which, there are Navajo clans whose traditions lay out connections with puebloan ancestors in convincing detail.

But turning ancestral puebloan remains over to the Navajo is not something that the Hopi and other contemporary pueblo groups find tolerable, so they've blasted the NPS's conclusion in no uncertain terms. The Navajo, seeing in the pueblo complaint an attack on their historical legitimacy, have fired back. The hapless Park Service is caught in the middle.

Now suppose we simply asked the Navajo and Hopi what they thought should be done with the ancestors—without quibbling about whose ancestors they are? I'm one hundred percent sure that their answers would be the same: the ancestors should go back into the ground. There might well be debate about *how* they should go back into the ground, and maybe about *where*, but such questions would not carry anything like the freight that's carried by questions of ownership. How to treat the dead respectfully, I feel sure, could be established through relatively calm negotiation.

But under NAGPRA, the NPS can't get to the point of negotiating about treatment until it has established who's sufficiently related to the ancestors in question to have a seat at the table. The NPS is blocked in getting to the resoluble issue of disposal by the probably irresoluble issue of "ownership."

Or consider the famous case of Kennewick Man.[3] A skeleton washes out of the bank of the Columbia River and falls into the hands of the property manager of the U.S. Army Corps of Engineers. In compliance with NAGPRA, the Corps sets out to establish ownership—i.e., cultural and genetic relationship—among the tribes of the area. But the bones turn out to be 11,000 years old, and to some physical anthropologists they don't look like those of a Native American ancestor; they look like those of a twenty-third-century starship captain. The physical anthropologists think this is pretty neat, so they want to keep the bones out of the ground. They challenge the tribes, and the Corps, to demonstrate that the dead guy is ancestral to *any* tribe. As this is written, the matter is still in court, unresolved after five years of tumult and shouting.

Now suppose the Corps didn't have to establish ownership, but only to come up with a way to treat Kennewick Man with the respect due a human being regardless of race, relationship, or Starfleet rank. It probably still wouldn't be easy—the tribes would certainly argue for prompt reburial; the physical anthropologists would certainly argue for perpetual storage and study. But at least they'd be arguing about real issues, and issues that might be amenable to resolution through thoughtful compromise. Agreement might well be reached on reburial after some amount of analysis, or on some other approach that, while not perfect from anybody's point of view, was at least acceptable to all. There wouldn't have to be winners and losers. But NAGPRA doesn't allow the Corps to do this. Under NAGPRA, somebody in the Kennewick controversy will win and somebody will lose. And the process of deciding who's the winner and who's the loser has generated great discord among people who should have common interests in protecting ancestral remains.

Could we develop a law based on respect for the dead, rather than on ownership? I think so. Such a law could simply articulate the principle of respect and lay out the basic range of treatments for the dead and their goods that flow from that principle. It could then direct agencies and museums to negotiate with tribes about how to treat ancestral remains in a manner consistent with such principles, leading to a binding and implemented agreement in each case. As with Section 106, where agreement was not reached, a representative body like the existing NAGPRA Review Committee might review the case and render a final binding decision or perhaps (as in Section 106) a nonbinding recommendation.

With sacred objects and objects of cultural patrimony, something more along the lines of NAGPRA might be necessary. Such objects are wanted by the tribes because they feel they are theirs; they are often wanted in order to put them to use; they are often perceived to have been stolen, and the obvious way to put this to rights is to give them back. Even with such objects, though, it might be useful to see how far one could get substituting respect and compromise for assertions of ownership. In some cases it's quite clear that sacred objects and objects of cultural patrimony were flatly stolen by collectors, anthropologists, or museums, or that they were sold by people who didn't have the right to sell them. But in lots of other cases the rights and wrongs are not so clear. I remember as a grad student being told by an eminent cultural anthropologist about how sometime in the 1950s he had broken into a roundhouse and taken a lot of ceremonial regalia, because he and all his colleagues believed that the tribe that owned the house was extinct. Shocking to us today, but at the time he was undoubtedly doing what he thought was right—saving pieces of the tribe's expressive culture that he believed would soon be lost forever, and that belonged, he honestly thought, to no living person or group. Why fight about whether he was (legally or morally) right or wrong? Why not promote respect and compromise? Maybe in some cases we don't need to establish ownership—or at least what amounts to fee-simple title. Maybe we could recognize joint ownership, split ownership, or negotiate cooperative management.

All this is entirely hypothetical, however; we have NAGPRA to live with now, and like it or not, arguments over ownership cannot be avoided. I only hope that over time, we can find ways to focus on NAGPRA's laudable intent and minimize contention over its specific provisions and its regrettable grounding in Euro-American property law.

Notes

1. ACHP 1988a.
2. ACHP 1988b.
3. Cf. Thomas 2001.

15

Stupid TCP Tricks

Introduction

W hat's a "TCP?" The acronym for "traditional cultural property," that's what. Which obviously begs a question. "Traditional cultural property," that oh-so-turgid term, was coined by Patricia L. Parker and me in the late 1980s during preparation of National Register *Bulletin* 38, *Guidelines for Evaluating and Documenting Traditional Cultural Properties.*[1] *Bulletin* 38 was published by the National Register of Historic Places in 1990. The acronym also works for "traditional cultural place," a term that means exactly the same thing but is sometimes used to avoid the implication of "property" that can be bought and sold.

But what does it mean? In *Bulletin* 38 we defined "traditional cultural property" as:

> (a place) that is eligible for inclusion in the National Register because of its association with cultural practices or beliefs of a living community that (a) are rooted in that community's history, and (b) are important in maintaining the continuing cultural identity of the community.[2]

This definition—being in a National Register publication—naturally emphasizes Register eligibility. However, in an educational videotape released in about 1995,[3] the National Register acknowledged that there may also be TCPs that are not strictly eligible for the National Register, but that are nevertheless culturally important places that need to be considered under laws other than the National Historic Preservation Act. A piece of the environment that's important to a community but hasn't had such importance long enough to make it eligible for the National Register might still need to be considered under the National Environmental Policy Act, for example, and perhaps under the American Indian Religious Freedom Act, Executive Order 12898, Executive Order 13007, or under an agency's own organic legislation.

Appropriately, perhaps, a good deal of folklore has grown up in the CRM world about TCPs, and there are now experts willing and anxious to propound all manner of rules about what TCPs are, what characteristics they must have, how they relate to the National Register Criteria, and so forth. The purpose of this chapter is to clarify a number of things about the TCP concept. Things that badly need clarifying, since people keep saying and writing such breathtakingly dumb things about it.

Of course, I have no official authority whatever to correct such errors, but I did coauthor the *Bulletin,* and I think I can speak with some confidence about what Dr. Parker and I were thinking when we wrote it. I've also watched, and experienced, the development of TCP practice over the last decade, and have kicked myself for some of the things we wrote and failed to write.

Following are some of the strange, silly, plain wrong, and in some (more interesting) cases simply debatable propositions about TCPs that I've run across over the course of the decade plus since *Bulletin* 38 burst upon the world.

It All Started in 1990 (or 1992)

It's not uncommon for writers to allege that TCPs "became eligible for the National Register" with issuance of *Bulletin* 38 in 1990—or when Congress amended the National Historic Preservation Act in 1992 to include Section 101(d)(6), which notes that American Indian and Native Hawaiian TCPs, at least, can be determined eligible.

Neither allegation is true. In fact, since *Bulletin* 38 itself gives examples of TCPs that were at the time of its writing included in the Register, it's obvious that the eligibility of such properties didn't begin with the Bulletin. I think that the notion of community cultural value as the basis for a property's historical significance was essential to the conception of the National Historic Preservation Act, and certainly places of traditional cultural significance were included in the Register from the time of its inception. As for the 1992 amendment, it resulted from the fact that when *Bulletin* 38 was issued three major federal agencies—the Bureau of Land Management, the Forest Service, and (somewhat ironically) the Bureau of Indian Affairs—issued guidance to their field offices saying that, as the *Bulletin* was a Park Service publication, it could be ignored. TCP aficionados who found this irritating prevailed upon Congress to clarify matters with Section 101(d)(6).

It's a New National Register Criterion

A twist on the "it all started in 1990" notion is the perception that the quality of being a TCP is somehow a new National Register criterion, added on to the four familiar criteria set forth at 36 CFR 60.4. This too is not true. To be eligible for the Register, a place has to meet one of the four standard Register criteria. Most often and most easily, TCPs are found eligible under Criterion "A," for their association with significant traditional events in the history (which may be folkloric) of the group that values them.

Actually, there is no necessary equation between being a TCP and being eligible for the National Register, any more than there is between being an archeological site and being eligible, or being a building and being eligible. National Register *Bulletin* 38 is of course a National Register publication, but so are (for example) *Bulletin* 20 on ships and shipwrecks and *Bulletin* 34 on aids to navigation. The fact that these property types are the subjects of National Register Bulletins doesn't mean that "ship" and "aid to navigation" are new National Register criteria. Nor does it mean that every ship and lighthouse is eligible for the Register; it just means that some are, and the Register felt that guidance was needed on how to determine which are and which aren't. The terms "ship" and "aid to navigation" were in common use before their *Bulletin* was written, of course, and "TCP" was not, but that's just an accident of history and semantics. A traditional cultural property is a kind of place, just like a lighthouse or a piece of vernacular architecture. Some are eligible for the National Register, some are not. To determine eligibility, you apply the National Register Criteria, just as you do to any other place you need to evaluate.

If It's Not Eligible for the Register, Federal Law Affords It No Protection

You see this a lot in reports of TCP studies stimulated by Section 106 compliance needs. It reflects a certain blindness that Section 106 practitioners develop no matter what kinds of properties they're studying.

It's accurate to say that if a TCP (or anything else) isn't eligible for the National Register then Section 106 affords it no "protection"—or consideration. But there are federal laws besides Section 106. NEPA, for example, and the American Indian Religious Freedom Act. There's Executive Order 12898, which calls on agencies to be careful about environmental impacts on the interests of low-income and minority communities, and there's Executive Order 13007, which deals specifically with "Indian sacred sites" on federal land, with nary a reference to the National Register.

It's certainly true, though, that Section 106 provides the most organized system for "protecting" places, to the extent consultation and Memoranda of Agreement about treatment are defined as "protective." It's for this reason that I recommend in most cases that agencies and communities alike agree to treat TCPs as eligible for the Register, even if there are legitimate arguments to be made against eligibility. Regarding a place as eligible makes it possible to use the Section 106 process to negotiate its treatment; viewing it as not eligible but maybe worth considering under another legal authority leaves one with only the courts as a venue for conflict resolution. Section 106 consultation is often frustrating, but I'd prefer it to court any day.

It Means "Indian Sacred Site"

It's easy to equate TCPs with Indian-sacred sites (or spiritual places, as some, including I, prefer, since "sacred" carries a lot of baggage), because most of the high-profile Section 106 TCP cases have involved such spiritually significant locales. All one has to do is read *Bulletin* 38, however, to learn that this isn't true. The bulletin includes illustrated examples of African American, German American, Chinese American, Chuukese, Shaker, Palauan, Hispanic American, and Yapese TCPs, and includes in its definition of the term examples like:

> A rural community whose organization, buildings and structures, or patterns of land use reflect the cultural traditions valued by its long-term residents;
>
> An urban neighborhood that is the traditional home of a particular cultural group; and
>
> A location where a community has traditionally carried out economic, artistic, or other cultural practices important in maintaining its historical identity.[4]

It's Only for Ethnic Communities

Well, OK, so it doesn't have to be "spiritual," or "sacred," but it does have to be important to some minority group, right?

Wrong. TCPs are for everyone. There's nothing in *Bulletin* 38 to suggest that plain old mainstream WASPs can't have TCPs. It's certainly a fact that we were motivated to write *Bulletin* 38 largely by the fact that places important to ethnic minorities (notably Indians, but others too; one of the cases that triggered the *Bulletin*'s production was destruction of a Polish American neighborhood in Detroit) were being given short shrift in project review. It's also true that minority groups, notably Indian tribes, have made a lot more use of *Bulletin* 38 than has anyone else, but TCPs are for everyone. *Bulletin* 38 explicitly says:

> Americans of every ethnic origin have properties to which they ascribe traditional cultural value, and if such properties meet the National Register criteria, they can and should (sic; see below) be nominated for inclusion in the National Register.[5]

It's Got To Be "Discrete"

Writers about TCPs often say, usually rather offhandedly, that a TCP must be a "discrete location." That doesn't seem to mean that it has to avoid divulging confidences, but that it must be sort of smallish—a definite, clearly definable piece of space.

When pressed, "discrete location" promoters sometimes fall back on "Step One" in the evaluation process laid out in *Bulletin* 38, which says that you've got to "ensure that the entity under consideration is a property."[6] Of course you do, if you're trying to show that the TCP is eligible for the National Register. It's the National Register of Historic *Places*, right? Places. Physical chunks of real estate. Ergo, properties. What we were trying to get at is that the Register is made up of places, not "intangible" things like ways of life or beliefs or dance forms. Those intangibles may be fundamental to making a property eligible—indeed, I don't think a property *can* be eligible without recourse to something intangible (What's "association" if not intangible?), but there has to be a place involved. There's nothing in *Bulletin* 38 that specifies a size limit, however, and some of the examples given—landscapes, for example, and "linkages" of sites, structures, and objects, are pretty loosely bounded kinds of things. Which brings us to a related, if somewhat better-grounded, myth:

It's Got to Have Boundaries

The National Register is hung up on boundaries. This results from its central purpose as a system for the permanent designation of places for commemoration and illustration of the past—places that are presumed likely to be plotted on master plans in the same way locally designated historic districts are. So National Register nomination forms require nominators to go into considerable detail to define and justify a property's boundaries, and there's a section of *Bulletin* 38 that addresses the topic—noting at the outset that defining a TCP's boundaries "can present considerable problems."[7]

The problems arise from the fact that many kinds of TCPs—notably Indian, Native Hawaiian, and other indigenous spiritual places—aren't easily bounded. Actually I think it's a rare TCP that *can* be easily bounded. Think about it for a moment. Imagine a place that's culturally important to you, the reader. A place that helps define your identity, a place you feel close to. Now think how you'd assign boundaries to it. Sometimes they're obvious—the walls of Grandma's kitchen—but often they're not. If your TCP is a headland where as a kid you sat and watched the whales go by and thought great thoughts, how far into the land and sea do its boundaries go? Can you decide? And what do we mean by boundaries, anyhow? Locations beyond which we don't care whether people build dams or tract houses, launch rockets, or detonate bombs? Or some kind of real estate division? If it's the latter, what's the point? If it's the former, aren't we really talking about an area of potential effect[8] rather than a property boundary?

So if you're nominating a TCP to the National Register, you're likely to have trouble with boundaries. Luckily, most communities aren't dumb enough to nominate their TCPs. Occasionally there's a good reason to, but usually there's not; it's just something the Register likes people to do. I strongly advice ignoring the Register's preferences in this matter. In most cases TCP issues come up in the context of Section 106 review, and in such cases there's seldom any reason to nominate anything. The Section 106 regulations specify that:

> If the agency Official determines any of the National Register Criteria are met and the SHPO/THPO agrees, the property shall be considered eligible for the National Register for section 106 purposes.[9]

An agency and SHPO or THPO can agree to *consider* a place eligible for the National Register for purposes of a given Section 106 case, based on whatever documentation they jolly well please. They're not bound by the requirements of National Register forms. So while it's a true fact that if we're going to nominate a TCP to the National Register, we're going to have to give it some boundaries, it is not true that we need to do so for purposes of considering it eligible under Section 106. We're free to decide whether it's useful to determine boundaries—whether doing so contributes to reaching decisions about effects and what to do about them. If it's useful, fine, define them; if it's not, don't waste time with them.

I don't mean to suggest that there are never occasions when it's important to define boundaries. Of course there are such occasions, just as there are occasions when it's important to figure out whether, say, the visual or auditory qualities of a place contribute to its significance. Arguably, very small impacts on a very big TCP are (at least sometimes) less damaging than big impacts on a small TCP, and if one is going to weigh and balance the severity of impacts one needs to have some idea how big the TCP is. And if we're talking about the kinds of effects that archeologists tend to be concerned about—bulldozing through a cemetery, say—it may be important to figure out where the physically threatened property begins and ends. I'm simply saying that one shouldn't think of boundaries as things that must be defined in all cases before one can decide that something's eligible and begin looking at effects and mitigation. Maybe boundaries are necessary, maybe they aren't. Look at the situation as it exists in the real world, not at the requirements imposed by the National Register on its rather otherworldly nomination process.

There Has to Have Been Continuous Use

Presumably based on *Bulletin* 38's language about a TCP having to be "important in maintaining the continuing cultural identity of the community,"[10] you sometimes find people—including National Register staffers, unfortunately—saying that to be eligible, a place must have been in some kind of continuous cultural use. Again, there's nothing in *Bulletin* 38 that says this. Consider Jerusalem. Was Jerusalem not an important traditional cultural property to Jews even when its occupation by Muslims and Christian crusaders made it difficult or impossible for them to live or worship there? Or the Sea of Galilee—how many devout Christians continue to "use" it in anything but a metaphorical sense? Now consider a Cherokee spiritual place in South Carolina, taken over by whites after Andrew Jackson and his cronies marched most of the Cherokee and their neighbors off to Oklahoma along the Trail of Tears. Is the Cherokee Nation of Oklahoma unable to assert the cultural importance of the place because they've been forcibly kept from using it all these years? Continuous (or discontinuous, or renewed) use is *one* thing that characterizes *some kinds* of TCPs, but it's hardly a defining characteristic of every such property.

It Has to Display Some Work of Human Beings

Few people who've even glanced at *Bulletin* 38 allege outright that there has to be something of human origin in order to make a TCP eligible, since the bulletin clearly says that:

119

Construction by human beings is a necessary attribute of buildings and structures, but districts, sites, and objects do not have to be the products of, or contain, the work of human beings in order to be classified as properties. . . . A culturally significant natural landscape may be classified as a site, as may the specific location where significant traditional events, activities, or cultural observances have taken place. A natural object such as a tree or rock outcrop may be an eligible object if it is associated with a significant tradition or use.[11]

However, it's still common enough for agencies, SHPOs, and consultants to *act* as though a place has to show the hand of Man in order to be eligible—for example, by holding that a place can't be regarded as eligible until an archeologist has gone out and "verified" it. When an agency official made such an assertion during a meeting on a controversial TCP a few years ago, he was asked just what he expected his archeologists to find. Sherds of significance? He couldn't answer, but clearly had never considered the possibility that a place could be eligible for the Register if his archeologists couldn't recognize it as such.

TCPs have to be physical pieces of property, but they do not have to show the work of human beings. They can be natural rocks, trees, forests, lakes, canyons, mountains. There doesn't have to be anything there that an archeologist, or architectural historian, or historian, or astronaut can recognize. What matters is what's seen, or otherwise experienced or believed, by the community that values the property. We don't send archeologists out to look for footprints on Galilee.

It Has to Be Documented Somewhere, At Least in Oral Tradition

This is a rather sticky one, about which Lynne Sebastian, erstwhile New Mexico SHPO, and I (among others) have sparred for years. Let's first consider the point on which I know Sebastian and I are in full agreement. It's *not* necessary for a TCP to be documented somewhere in the Euro-American literature—in an ethnography, or a history, or an explorer's account, in order to be eligible. *Bulletin* 38 points out that there are lots of reasons a place may not be mentioned in the literature:

Ethnographic and ethnohistorical research has not been conducted uniformly in all parts of the nation. . . .

The fact that (a document) does not identify a property as culturally important may reflect only the fact that the individual who prepared the report had research interests that did not require the identification of such properties.

Some kinds of traditional cultural properties are regarded by those who value them as the loci of supernatural or other power, or as having other attributes that make people reluctant to talk about them.[12]

To which we can add the fact that maybe nobody ever asked the people about the place.

Where Sebastian and I part company is over the matter of oral tradition. Sebastian (with others) has argued that for a place to be a National Register–eligible TCP there has to be traditional knowledge of the place, so if the place isn't known to the community, it can't be a TCP—or at least a TCP that's eligible for the National Register.[13]

It seems to me that it comes down to how specifically a community needs to know a place. As I understand her, Sebastian would require that the community know that Place X, with Y kind of significance, exists more or less in Location Z. She would allow for the fact that for many generations a community might have been unable to visit Location Z, and hence could be kind of fuzzy about exactly where it is or what Place X looks like, but the community ought to have some idea that something of a more or less known character is out there in a more or less known general area. This all seems very reasonable, but I disagree.

Consider the Hopi. In Hopi tradition, the ancestors traveled widely over the Southwestern United States before settling on the Hopi Mesas where they have resided for the last several centuries. Some specific locations are mentioned in tradition, but undoubtedly the ancestors stopped, had experiences, and lived for periods of time at many locations whose specific identities have been lost. Does this mean that when such a location is found today, for example by a Hopi elder accompanying an archeological survey team, it does not have traditional cultural significance? If so, it seems terribly arbitrary to me. Why should we not say that according to Hopi tradition, the ancestors traveled through the area, and places associated with them are culturally significant because of that association—whether a given specific place is mentioned in a specific tradition or not? And as for Register eligibility, do the travels of the Hopi ancestors not comprise a significant pattern of events, association with which in the eyes of the Hopi makes properties eligible under Criterion (a)?

Or consider the African Burial Ground (ABG) in New York City, discovered a few years ago during a construction project. Everybody had forgotten the burial ground since it was abandoned sometime in the early nineteenth century and it had been built over as Manhattan Island urbanized. It certainly did not figure in the oral or written traditions of the African American community of New York City or anyplace else. Yet when it was discovered there was tremendous excitement and concern about what was happening to it that resulted in a congressional investigation, major modifications to the project plans, and the expenditure of millions of dollars both in penalty payments to the construction contractor and in research costs. The ABG is now a National Historic Landmark, which will be marked with a memorial building once those buried there are reinterred. Is the ABG not a TCP? Does it not have cultural importance to African Americans, simply because they didn't remember it during the somewhat tumultuous decades of the nineteenth and twentieth centuries? It had cultural significance when it was in use, and it has cultural significance now that it's been rediscovered; the fact that white society in effect took it away from the community during the intervening years, both physically and as a place-specific memory, doesn't seem to me to diminish its relevance to the African American traditional culture.

So I'd agree with Sebastian to the extent of saying that if the Hopi had no tradition of ancestral wanderings through the Southwest, or if there were no tradition (or written history) of enslaved Africans in New York City, one couldn't have Hopi or African American TCPs there. But I see no reason to insist that a community's traditions mention a specific place in order for that place, when found, to be recognized by the community as having cultural significance.

It Can't Be "Mitigated," but Must Be "Avoided"

This is something you hear a lot from tribes. You can't *mitigate* our spiritual places; you have to *avoid* them. It makes a certain amount of sense, but only when you recognize that the tribe is using archeo-talk.

Mitigation, of course, is something that exists with respect to circumstances, or effects, or other things that *happen*. One can't *mitigate sites*, or buildings, or people, or planets. But to a lot of archeologists, "mitigation" means "digging." Doing archeological data recovery; excavating sites and translating them into reports and museum collections. A lot of tribes have been introduced to federal CRM systems by archeologists; as a result they may fall into archeo-jargon. So what a tribe really means when it says "You can't mitigate our spiritual place," may very well be that "You can't make adverse effect on our spiritual place go away by digging it up."

Avoid, in this context, is also archeo-talk. "Avoiding a site" to an archeologist equals "avoiding effect on it." You put the road over there, beyond the boundary of the site, rather than through it, and you've avoided effect by avoiding the site. This is fine from an archeological standpoint, because the only effect an archeologist is concerned about is physical effect on the site's deposits. But it's not necessarily fine from the point of view of a tribe, whose members may be concerned about visual, audible, atmospheric, social, spiritual—all kinds of effects. The road may avoid the site, but the noise from the road will still have an effect on the integrity of the site as a place of worship, or it may scare away the spirit beings that make the place important.

So it's important to understand that when a tribe (or a tribe's archeologist) says "you can't mitigate, you've got to avoid," what's said is probably both less and more than what's meant. Less because it may very well be possible to "mitigate" impacts on the site, by relocating the road over the hill, or providing visual or noise buffers, or using the road only during the season when there aren't ceremonies going on at the site, or making a financial contribution to the tribal traditional medicine fund. More because in order to achieve such mitigation it may not be necessary—or sufficient—to avoid the site. Physical avoidance may, in fact, be irrelevant; putting the road right next to the site may be just as bad as putting it right through it.

When assertions like this one get tossed around, as they often do in Section 106 consultation, they can really seem like show stoppers, but they don't need to be. It's important to look behind the rhetoric and try to figure out what people are really talking about. There may be lots more opportunities for compromise than the hard (and inaccurate) rhetoric suggests.

Obviously the "no mitigation/must avoid" rhetoric is code for "don't do your project here," but that doesn't necessarily mean "don't do your project anywhere," or even "don't do your project here with X, Y, and Z adjustments." The tribe may not—very probably has not—thought about where it *would be* OK to do your project, or what adjustments might make it acceptable. The first response to something one doesn't like is usually simply to say "no," and many tribal people have trouble understanding why that flat rejection isn't enough by itself to make a project proponent go away. "We've told you and told you and told you," the elder will scold, "we don't *want* this project!" So it may be hard to prevail upon a tribe's representatives to think about alternatives and a full range of mitigation measures. But if one works at it, respectfully, exploring what the tribe means by "avoid" and "mitigate," and posing alternatives for consideration, it may well be possible to work out a resolution that everyone can be satisfied with.

It Requires "100 Percent Survey"

When you hear someone—usually a tribe—propose that a "100 percent TCP survey" is needed, it's another case in which you have to understand that the speaker has fallen into archeo-talk. A lot of archeologists do "100 percent survey." Some even think it's required by law or regulation. Exactly what it means varies. Some people focus on the end result, and say it means that you've inspected the area (whatever the area is) in enough detail to find "all the sites." Others recognize this as silly (you can never be sure you've found "all the sites"), and focus on means: a 100 percent survey is where you've had archeologists look carefully at 100 percent of the area.

There's some logic (not much, in my opinion) to the idea that some sort of 100 percent survey is needed to identify archeological sites. It's not sufficient to identify all such sites (you need background research too, and consultation with knowledgeable local people), and in my view it's by no means always justified, but there's some logic to it. Archeologists find sites by observing them, and noting that they have certain characteristics that say "site" to archeologists. There's rather less logic in applying the same standard to TCPs, and I doubt if most tribes would propose such a standard if they hadn't encountered a lot of archeologists doing such surveys, and decided that they wanted parity.

Certainly having a knowledgeable person—a tribal elder, for example—go out in the field and look around can be a very useful thing to do as part of an effort to locate TCPs, but it's only part of the picture. Talking to the elders is really the point—having them say what's important. If this can be done in the field it's usually best, but if it can't, that doesn't mean one's survey is flawed. Background research is also tremendously important in TCP identification. Detailed survey to inspect every piece of the ground is a whole lot less important, because TCPs usually don't yield themselves up to visual identification the way archeological sites do. If Elder X doesn't tell you that Boxed-In Canyon is a place of great spiritual power, you're probably not going to find that out by going there and inspecting the ground. You may go there and experience some sort of power, but does that experience demand spreading people out over the landscape and making sure every foot of ground is looked at? I can't see why it should.

The identification standard for TCPs, as for every other kind of historic property under Section 106, is that one make a "reasonable and good faith effort" to find them. Those who insist on 100 percent survey need to be able to explain why this is a reasonable strategy. The fact that archeologists do it isn't sufficient.

The Problem of "Community"

Throughout this chapter, and throughout *Bulletin* 38, the term "community" is thrown around pretty loosely. Just what *is* a community? And how big does it have to be?

Suppose, for example, that a single (that is, by himself or herself, not necessarily unmarried) individual asserts that there's an important spiritual place up that canyon, so you'd better not build the road there. Is the individual a community? Can the canyon be eligible for the National Register based on his say-so?

It's a sticky question. Easy to say "No, a community must have multiple members," but what if the individual is the last member of a once-thriving group? Or what if there still is a group, but the individual is the last of its traditional elders, the only one who remembers anything about the old ways, the old beliefs? And isn't the individual an American citizen, who's entitled to respect?

And of course, what if it's not just one person, but two or three? On the other hand, what if the group that claims to be a community isn't a well-defined formal group like an Indian tribe, but an organization made up, say, of people from a dozen Indian tribes, a couple of Native Hawaiian families, and some white hangers-on?

I don't think there's a good answer to this question. When I've run into it, my tendency has been to say "OK, let's assume for the sake of argument that you're a community, and trust your evaluation of this site. Where does that lead us?" Often enough, once one gets past the question of whether there's an eligible property involved, and makes everybody understand that you're not going to belittle them and insist that they have no standing, everyone can sit down and work out practical ways to address treatment of the place.

But what if there's no agreement on treatment measures? What if push comes to shove and the only way to address the alleged significance of the place is to cancel the project whose review under Section 106 has brought everybody to the table? Here, I think the level of evidence required must be ratcheted up; one has to ask whether the individual asserting the significance of the place represents anybody other than himself, as well as whether there's any reason external to him to accept his allegations about the place's significance. In other words, I'd let anybody and everybody come to the table and make their assertions about the significance of places threatened by the project, and I'd try to find ways to accommodate everybody's needs. But if that didn't work; if the only way to accommodate the stated needs of the individual claiming significance for the site was to deny another party—like the project proponent—the fulfillment of its needs, then I'd need to look for validation of the individual's claims. And this would usually include seeing whether there really was a larger community that shared the individual's beliefs. But at the beginning of consultation I certainly would not try to exclude people and their views because I didn't think they represented "communities," or for that matter because I thought they had their own agendas, their own axes to grind, or because I thought they were lying through their teeth. Being taken seriously, being respected, can work wonders as a means of encouraging agreement.

Seeking agreement is in the end what Section 106 is about, and the reason we wrote *Bulletin* 38 was to ensure that communities that were being ignored in the Section 106 process—including, conceivably, communities of one—got the opportunity to come to the table and negotiate with everyone else. *Bulletin* 38 wasn't designed to ensure that TCPs are always protected or given some kind of consideration at a higher level than that given other kinds of historic properties. It was designed simply to ensure that the professional historians, archeologists, and architects who carry out most Section 106 review didn't ignore the concerns of real people, in real communities, about places that are important to them. My general advice is not to split hairs about whether something technically meets the precise standards of every arguably applicable National Register Bulletin. If somebody says it's significant, assume it is, and see where you can go based on that assumption. The results can be surprising, and gratifying all around. The results of trying to exclude people's concerns through narrow interpretation of regulations and guidelines are almost sure to be something else entirely.

Notes

I am grateful to Dr. Lynne Sebastian for critical comments on a draft of this essay, but nothing in it should be taken to reflect Dr. Sebastian's opinions.

1. Parker and King 1990 (Bulletin 38).

2. *Bulletin* 38:1.

3. *Through the Generations: Identifying and Protecting Traditional Cultural Places.* National Register of Historic Places and Department of Agriculture, Natural Resources Conservation Service, with the Advisory Council on Historic Preservation, National Conference of State Historic Preservation Officers. No date given on tape, but approximately 1995.

4. *Bulletin* 38:1.

5. *Bulletin* 38:3.

6. *Bulletin* 38:9.

7. *Bulletin* 38:18.

8. Defined at 36 CFR 800.16(d) as "the geographic area or areas within which (a Federal action) may directly or indirectly cause changes in the character or use of historic properties, if any such properties exist."

9. 36 CFR 800.4(c)(2).

10. *Bulletin* 38:1.

11. *Bulletin* 38:9.

12. *Bulletin* 38:8.

13. Most recently articulated in an Internet discussion conducted by Jeani L. Borchert of North Dakota, on ACRA-L, August 2, 2001.

16

Bigger than a Breadbox?

How big can a traditional cultural property be? It's generally understood that some of them, particularly Native American spiritual places, can be pretty large—whole mountains, ridges, lakes, valleys—but there's also a good deal of discomfort among CRM practitioners about TCPs that are "too big."

Of course, scale issues are not unique to TCPs. Cultural landscapes, battlefields, urban and rural historic districts can all be pretty good sized. But people seem to experience particular kinds of angst about big TCPs and want to break them up into smaller pieces. The lake is regarded as spiritually significant? Tough; we've got to find something smaller on its shore—a rock or a cove or a fishing area—to be eligible for the National Register.

In fact, though, the National Register regulations place no size limits on National Register properties; the only real questions pertinent to eligibility are: does the place meet any of the National Register Criteria, and does it retain integrity? Some pretty large places can easily meet those standards.

Consider, for example, the Grand Canyon, where a couple of years ago I was part of a group that looked into how the Bureau of Reclamation and National Park Service were doing their preservation work. The NPS had contracted with several of the tribes in the area to conduct TCP studies, and the tribes had identified side canyons, caves, salt deposits, crossings, plant gathering areas, and many other locations, associated with origin stories, traditional activities, traditional historical events, and so on. Every one of the tribes also said that the whole canyon, as such, figured importantly in their traditions and worldviews. They cited specific traditions to back up their statements.

There was a great deal of hand-wringing about which arroyos, rocks, and caves might be eligible for the Register and why, and what their boundaries might be, but we finally tumbled to the fact that the whole Grand Canyon is obviously eligible for the National Register. The individual sites are simply contributing elements, if you will—like architectural elements in a building, or individual buildings in an urban district.

This realization resolved a lot of problems. We no longer had to worry about whether all the significant TCPs had been identified, or what their boundaries were, or how to rationalize their eligibility (or ineligibility) under the National Register Criteria. We could simply accept them all as elements of the great big eligible property and get on to the important, real world question of how to manage them. But the idea of viewing the whole canyon as eligible was still pretty hard for people to swallow—though no one, in my hearing, could quite say why. It just seemed too big. Some management concern sprang from the assumption that recognizing the whole thing as eligible would increase the level of need for or complexity of Section 106 review, but most people eventually came to see that review would actually be simplified. If it wasn't necessary to do studies to apply the National Register Criteria to potentially affected rocks, waterfalls, and archeological sites, or to argue about eligibility, the process of review could—in theory at least—be considerably streamlined. Always recalling, of course—and this was probably what Management didn't quite understand, and what made the "Whole Eligible Canyon" notion uncomfortable to them—that Section 106 doesn't prohibit anyone from doing anything; they just have to consider the impacts of doing it. The NPS could fill in the Canyon and make it into a golf course if it wished; it would just have to review the historic preservation impacts of doing so. And that review would be simplified by seeing the whole thing as eligible.

The advantage in the Grand Canyon instance, though, was that all the land involved (or virtually all of it) was either federal or tribal land. Things get more complicated when other kinds of land are involved, as I learned when I was engaged by the Bad River and Red Cliff Bands of

Chippewa to help assess the eligibility of Chequamegon Bay, on the southwest shore of Lake Superior, for the National Register.[1] The Bay, it turned out, was clearly eligible—though a consultant for a change agent in the area had insisted that there were no "specific" eligible sites around its shores. But it also quickly became apparent that something bigger was also eligible—Lake Superior.

Both the pertinent literature and the testimony of tribal members indicated that in Chippewa tradition the whole of Lake Superior has spiritual importance. Lake Superior was and is regarded by traditional Chippewa as a spiritual phenomenon, both in itself and as the home of powerful spirits. The whole lake is identified as the Great Medicine Lodge or *Midewegun*,[2] shelter and ultimate origin place of the ancestors. It is the place where many of the adventures of the culture hero *Wenabojo* took place. In traditions central to the identity of the Chippewa and their traditional *Mide* religion, the ancestors migrated along its shores from a place on the salt sea in the east, following the sacred *megis* shell. And of course, it was and is a major source of sustenance for Chippewa people. Although there are lots of smaller places on and around and under the lake that are culturally significant, these don't detract from the cultural significance of the lake itself, as a whole. Rather, they contribute to it.

A number of the elders and others who advised me clearly thought that I should say in my report that the whole lake was eligible. When I looked at the issue, on purely intellectual grounds I couldn't disagree. Lake Superior meets at least National Register Criterion A, for its traditional cultural associations as well as for its association with more recent historical events. As for integrity, this is very much in the eye of the beholder. In the eyes of traditional Chippewa who regard the whole lake as "sacred," it must retain integrity or they would not continue to regard it so.

But if Lake Superior is eligible for the National Register, I thought, would we not have to say that the entire North American continent, or the whole world, is eligible? We probably could, but the logic for doing so would not be as sound as that for regarding Superior as eligible. Lake Superior is a coherent—albeit large—geographic feature: a basin filled with water, with tributaries and outlets. It has a certain cultural coherency, too: Although the Chippewa are not the only cultural group associated with the great lake, they are one of a few such groups, whereas North America has cultural associations with all resident groups, both native and immigrant. And to the Chippewa, the Lake qua Lake, in its entirety, was and is visualized as the Great *Midewegun*. Some tribes talk about North America, under various traditional names, as a single traditional place, too, and in many ways it is so in the eyes of mainstream U.S. and Canadian culture, but it doesn't have the sort of links to traditions, by name, that Lake Superior possesses. I could find ways to argue that North America is not eligible for the Register; I couldn't find any basis other than my discomfort with its size for saying that Lake Superior isn't.

The practical ramifications of an eligibility determination were awesome, however—far, far more imposing than those of regarding the Grand Canyon as eligible. It wasn't a matter of the lake being "too big"—it was the simple, practical fact that a proposal for any sort of formal eligibility determination would be wildly misunderstood and generate pointless controversy. People would immediately assume that the NPS or some other fearsome entity of Government was taking the first steps toward declaring the whole lake a National Monument and bringing it into the National Park System. It would be assumed that recognizing its eligibility would stop commerce on the lake, interfere with private property rights, and generally be economically and socially burdensome. To some extent these fears would be justified, though not under federal law. Federal law would merely require that the cultural significance of the lake be taken into account when considering federal actions that might affect it, and in theory Federal agencies are required to do this whether the Lake had been previously recognized as eligible or not. Some state laws, however, are more draconian, actually limiting what a private property owner can do with a property determined eligible for the Register. Such laws reflect the confusion I've discussed (perhaps overmuch) in other essays between the Register's role as a list of the "best and brightest" and its role in establishing a threshold for consideration in agency planning. Confused or not, such laws exist, and determining the lake eligible for the Register could trigger their application, with quite unpredictable consequences.

In the end, I reached a rather messy conclusion that reflected reality as I understood it. Lake Superior probably *is* eligible for the National Register, but I did not recommend that it be "officially" determined so on behalf of the federal government. Rather, I suggested, agencies should simply recognize the lake's cultural, spiritual significance to the Chippewa (and perhaps others) when carrying out Section 106 review. They should consult with affected groups to see how these aspects of significance may be affected, and seek ways to mitigate effects that are adverse. In other words, they should do basically what they're supposed to do anyway under Section 106 (and other authorities), but they needn't waste their time on arguments about the lake's eligibility. Accept it as such and proceed from there. Formally *determining* the lake eligible, however, was something I did not recommend. It would, I felt, result in procedural nightmares at the state and local levels and wouldn't accomplish anything at the federal level.

All of which leads me to the conclusion that, yes, TCPs are often quite large, and that's simply the nature of the beasts; it's pointless and a waste of time to try to reduce them, or atomize them. But at the same time, there are often practical impediments to recognizing the eligibility of really big ones for the National Register. Luckily under Section 106 we have the option of considering places eligible without making any kind of formal determination. With big TCPs, that's an option we should probably employ more often than not.

Notes

1. King 1999.
2. C.f. Dewdney 1975:74–6.

17

*What Should We Consult about, and How Much Information Do We Need to Do It?**

Introduction

Consultation about how to address the effects of a federal action on historic properties is at the core of the process of project review under Section 106 of the National Historic Preservation Act. Consultation with Indian tribes and others in the course of Section 106 review is explicitly required by Sections 101(d)(6)(B) and 110(a)(2)(E) of the same act.

The way the Section 106 process is commonly practiced, however, can actually throw up roadblocks to effective consultation, particularly where tribal cultural values and historic properties are involved. What are these roadblocks, and how can they be overcome or circumnavigated?

What is "Effective Consultation"?

In the words of the Section 106 regulations, "consultation" means:

> The process of seeking, discussing, and considering the views of other participants, and, where feasible, seeking agreement with them. (36 CFR 800.16(f))

---

*Presented at a symposium on "Managing the Cultural Landscape through Consultation" at the Annual Meeting of the Society for American Archaeology, 2001.

- "Process"—not a meeting, a notice, a particular thing one does, but a process of . . .

- "Seeking"—actually trying to find out what people think.

- "Considering"—actually thinking about it.

- "Discussing"—a dialogue, a reasoning together.

- "Seeking agreement"—trying to come to a mutually agreeable conclusion.

Consultation under Section 106, in other words, is supposed to be a back-and-forth conversation or negotiation, involving multiple interested parties (however many there may be), that attempts to reach agreement. A consultation is effective, I think, if it leads to agreement, or at least to a decision that all participants can agree has been reached fairly, with full consideration of everyone's views.

The best kind of negotiation I know of is what some alternative dispute resolution experts[1] call "principled negotiation." Principled negotiation involves a deliberate effort to maintain openness and flexibility, to put oneself in the other party's shoes, to consider interests and issues and avoid getting hung up on establishing and defending positions. It's aimed at achieving mutual gain where possible. An important feature of principled negotiation is to avoid playing games, to avoid forcing people into structures that impede their formulation and open consideration of alternatives. To work it's got to be flexible, fluid, and try to address everybody's issues honestly.

I think that most of us can agree that consultation under Section 106 should be carried out along such lines. Assuming that it reflects respect for tribal sovereignty and cultural sensitivity, I think principled negotiation is the way to carry out consultation with tribes under Section 106. But traditionally, it's not always, or even often, the way Section 106 review is done.

The "Traditional" Way of Doing Section 106 Review

By *traditional* I do not mean traditional to a tribe, or traditional to principled negotiation, but traditional to Section 106 review as practiced by

135

many State Historic Preservation Officers (SHPOs) and Section 106 consultants, as implicitly encouraged by some of the direction provided by the Advisory Council on Historic Preservation, and as explicitly promoted by the National Park Service in its oversight of SHPO programs. "Traditional" Section 106 consultation is organized as follows:

1. Although the Section 106 regulations, at 36 CFR 800.3 and 800.4(a), encourage broad consultation during an agency's initiation of the review process and during early scoping, most agencies consult primarily if not solely with the SHPO or THPO at this stage. Such consultation often has a pro-forma character: the agency asks the SHPO/THPO if he or she knows of any historic properties that may be affected, and may ask for advice about what kind of identification to do. The subject of consultation is usually limited to identification, except to the extent that project effects may be predicted in order to establish the area of potential effects within which identification will be done.

2. The project proponent then goes out and does identification, often following some "standard" system recommended (or "required," in the eyes of the proponent) by the SHPO/THPO. Since SHPOs and THPOs have limited time and personnel, these systems are often formulistic, designed to be imposed automatically, by rote. One does a "Phase One" or "Class One" survey to identify properties, then a "Phase Two" or "Class Two" survey to evaluate them, and so on. These systems are almost invariably the creations of archeologists, and as a result cause identification to be narrowly focused on areas of direct project ground disturbance and on the kinds of historic properties an archeologist can recognize. If consultation (with tribes or others) takes place during identification, it is entirely about identification. "Do you have any sacred sites within these boundaries?" "Can you help us document TCPs?" "What can you tell us about this site we've found?"

3. Next comes evaluation, in which a professional—it certainly must be a professional, the National Register insists—decides

whether each place found during identification may be eligible for the National Register, and if so what characteristics contribute to its eligibility, and what Register Criteria apply. If consultation occurs at this stage, these are its subjects.

4. Next, the proponent and SHPO/THPO (and perhaps others) consult about whether the proposed action that's the subject of review will adversely affect the eligible properties. Here again there are formulae to apply, which are linked back to Register eligibility: will the project change what makes the property eligible for the Register, in a manner that will diminish its integrity? Pretty esoteric, often nitpicky, stuff.

5. Finally, assuming it's determined that there will be an adverse effect, consultation proceeds about how to "resolve" it, usually resulting in a Memorandum of Agreement.

How "Traditional" Section 106 Review Thwarts Effective Consultation

The rigid stepwise character of the process outlined above makes Section 106 review rather mysterious to the average person, and particularly so to many Native American communities. The need to gather information at each step—particularly during identification and evaluation—can also discourage tribes from participating, because it requires disclosure of information that many feel strongly should (even must) be kept confidential. It makes it very difficult to carry out the kind of flexible discussions, aimed at achieving mutual gain, that principled negotiation calls for.

Imagine the case of, say, a pipeline that's proposed through the aboriginal lands of a tribe. Suppose the tribe is concerned about the project because of its potential impacts on medicinal plants, several spiritually important springs, and a grove of trees in which the dead used to be exposed on scaffolds. Suppose the tribe wants to consult with the relevant parties about ways to reduce, avoid, compensate for, or otherwise mitigate these potential impacts. How does it do so?

Recognizing that it should get into consultation as early as possible— I realize that in the real world the tribe may not even know about the project until rather late in the planning process, but let's pretend—the tribe tells the proponent agency that it wants to be a part of Section 106 review starting at the very beginning of the process. The agency agrees. But please, tribe, you have to understand that all we're consulting about right now is how to do our identification. So if you can tell us about specific places that are important to you, fine, we'll have our archeologists check them out. Or maybe you can suggest what sort of survey strategy we should use, or even come into the field and show us places that you value.

Of course, the tribe may very well not want to identify such places. It may be barred by strong cultural norms from talking about them to outsiders, or it just may not trust the bastards. It may want to talk about how effects can be avoided on places it knows about but doesn't want to reveal, or on values in the landscape that are not specific to narrowly defined places. Well, sorry, tribe, it's premature to talk about effects. The regulations, we're quite sure, require us first to identify all the historic properties, as specifically and thoroughly as we can, so if you could please tell us . . .

The tribe and the agency are obviously talking past each other here—not because either intends to be obscure or difficult, but because the agency perceives the Section 106 regulations to require a step-by-step approach that precludes addressing the tribe's interests up front. The agency also is focusing its attention solely on historic properties, rather than on the general cultural-environmental effects of its project, and it assumes that to "take into account" the effects of its action on historic properties, it must first identify them all. The tribe isn't segregating out historic properties from the overall cultural-religious values they see in the environment, and they don't see why they have to reveal information about specific places in order to get the agency to pay attention to tribal concerns.

Assuming the tribe doesn't throw up its collective hands and walk away, the same problem will continue to trouble the "consulting" parties as identification proceeds. The agency will want to talk about property locations, site boundaries, physical attributes that make places significant, all of which may be very uncomfortable for the tribe to discuss. Those doing the identification—who are researchers, after all, whose primary orientation is toward the collection and analysis of data—will want to establish in the hardest, most "scientific" way possible just what's in the project's area of potential effect, and what makes each particular district, site, building, structure or object significant or insignificant. Until it has completed identification, the agency may well feel unable to discuss effects, particularly about effects on the overall cultural environment and how to avoid them.

When the consultation process turns to evaluation, the communication problems are likely to be magnified. Medicinal plants? Well, er, how long have you been gathering plants there? Over fifty years? How big is the area? Springs? What makes them significant? What kinds of spirits are in them? What do you do there? What are the boundaries? Scaffolds in trees? Well, let's dig to see if there are bones in the ground, or maybe core the trees to see if they're old enough to have been around back when scaffold burial was the practice. Which National Register criterion applies here, anyhow? Is medicinal plant gathering an important historical pattern with which this area may be associated under Criterion A? Do scaffolds constitute a type of architecture that's eligible under Criterion C? Can we study the scaffold burial site, or interview the spirits in the springs, to get information important in history or prehistory? If this sort of thing isn't flatly offensive to the tribe, it's at least likely to be incomprehensible, and thoroughly irrelevant.

If consultation gets as far as talking about effects, the situation will not be significantly improved, because to apply the Criterion of Adverse Effect at 36 CFR 800.5(a)(1) to each specific property, the agency's experts are going to want to figure out what characteristics contribute to the property's eligibility, and what gives these elements integrity. So the agency is right back to questioning the tribe about what makes the springs important to its traditional people and to debating whether if the trees in the grove are the distant descendants of those that held the scaffolds, the grove has lost integrity. The tribe, by now, is thoroughly confused at best. And of course, the agency will feel compelled to focus its consultation on specific effects on specific eligible properties. Broader effects, it will likely say, ought to be considered under the National Environmental Policy Act (NEPA), or the American Indian Religious Freedom Act (AIRFA), or something, not under Section 106.

Finally, consultation may turn to resolving adverse effects—provided some are acknowledged to exist. But by this time the nature of the effects may be so tightly constrained by transit through the previous steps that there's no way of really addressing the effects that matter. Consultation may focus on reducing physical damage to the grove, when the tribe is most concerned about messing up the aquifer that feeds the springs. It may home in on data recovery in the dirt around the trees, when it's the trees themselves that the tribe regards as significant, and the noise of construction that's the biggest perceived impact. The medicinal plants have probably already been excluded from the process because it's too hard to establish the boundaries that the National Register insists that every eligible property must have.

The result, if there is a result, is a Memorandum of Agreement that primarily addresses things that aren't very important to the tribe, while the things that *are* important are left to the uncertain mercies of NEPA and AIRFA. Another result, of course, is likely to be frustration and disgust on the part of the tribe.

None of this, I submit, is the fault of the agency. None of it is even the fault of the basic Section 106 process. It *is* the fault of the way the process is widely understood—as a rigid, stepwise procedure that requires gathering a lot of data to satisfy the predilections of academic researchers. And it's the fault of the National Register with its fixation on nomination-style documentation.

Another Way

There is a better way to do Section 106 consultation, that's perfectly permissible under the regulations. Using it requires a degree of creativity and flexibility, however, and it doesn't provide all the comfort that a rigid process gives to those who are challenged by ambiguity.

The key to using this process is to go back to the statute. Section 106, remember, requires agencies to "take into account the effects" of their actions on historic properties. Consultation should focus on effects and how to deal with them; identification and documentation of historic properties are only means to this end. We need to constantly remind ourselves of the direction that Lynne Sebastian gave us when she was New Mexico's SHPO: "Don't tell me anything I don't need to know to do my job." And our jobs are figuring out how to resolve adverse effects, not collecting the information needed to make the National Register and its defenders feel warm and fuzzy.

Suppose that our pipeline agency—very early in planning, in early coordination with NEPA, when lots of alternatives are available—contacts the tribe in a proper government-to-government way and asks if the tribe has any concerns about, among other things, impacts on the cultural environment.

Yes we do, says the tribe. We're concerned about impacts on these trees, these springs, and our ability to gather medicinal plants we need for our healing practices.

OK, says the agency, let's talk about that. This alternative over here would miss the trees, but it would take more medicinal plants. But could we transplant some plants, or help you acquire access to some land that's got good plants on it that you can't get to now? As for the springs, how about if we work with your tribal water quality people to find ways to make sure we don't mess up the aquifer?

Consultation proceeds, and an agreement is reached. A Memorandum of Agreement is prepared and signed. What does it say? Basically:

Whereas the agency, SHPO/THPO, tribe, etc. agree that the grove, the springs, and the landscape in which the plants grow may be eligible for the National Register, and

Whereas they've considered the effects of the pipeline on them,

Now, therefore, it's mutually agreed that the agency will use alternative B to avoid damage to the grove, purchase an easement on the tribe's behalf to plant-rich land parcel X in order to compensate for loss of medicinal plants, and employ measures 1, 2, and 3 to minimize impacts on the aquifer.

Everybody signs, the project proceeds. Everybody's happy.

But . . .

Let me quickly respond to some obvious objections.

- *It won't always work:* True. The kind of approach advocated above won't work in every case. For example, in a case where the agency proposes to take a controversial action—adopt an alternative that gores the ox of somebody other than the tribe, for example, or that has serious environmental impacts—based on the tribe's cultural concerns, the agency is going to need a detailed administrative record to support its decision, and that will require more detailed documentation of potential effects on cultural resources. The exact character of this record will depend on the nature of the project, the area, the resources, and the controversy. But I think the approach outlined here—and variations on the theme, of course—will work in a great many cases, and will greatly simplify consultation and make it more sensitive to tribal concerns in such cases. This is nothing to be sneezed at.

- *It addresses only resources known to tribes and important to them.* True again. There might still be a need for more "traditional" archeological surveys and such to identify resources important to other people, or even to tribes themselves. But with these re- sources, too, focusing on effects and away from eligibility could simplify consultation considerably. Are we likely to affect ar- chaic coprolite mounds or colonial revival gas stations? Fine, let's assume their eligibility and establish up front how they're going to be treated.

- *It's not consistent with the regulations.* Oh, but it is. The regula- tions require agencies to make a "reasonable and good faith ef- fort" to identify historic properties. They do not require agen- cies to identify every property in minute detail. They cite the Secretary of the Interior's *Standards for Identification* as guid- ance.

The very first of the Secretary's Standards says that:

Identification of historic properties is undertaken to the degree required to make decisions.[2]

The regulations allow agencies and SHPOs or THPOs to determine the eligibility of properties by consensus. In the case hypothesized above, the parties have reached consensus that the grove, the springs, and the landscape containing the medicinal plants are eligible. There's nothing in the regulations that requires us to agonize over boundaries, property types, levels of significance, or any of the other esoteric matters called for in National Register nomination forms. Sure, the National Register prefers that we do, and pressures the SHPOs to insist on it, but it's not required, and SHPOs do not have to give way to the Register's bullying.

The regulations require that agencies and other consulting parties ap- ply the Criteria of Adverse Effect. OK, if the pipeline goes through the trees that will be an adverse effect; it will diminish the integrity of the grove in the eyes of those who value it. Likewise if it causes the springs to dry up or impedes the traditional use of the medicinal plant landscape. There; we've applied the Criteria of Adverse Effect.

Finally, the regulations require consultation to resolve adverse effects. That's what's been done in the example above.

In Conclusion

Let me stress again that the sort of flexible, early, low-information, effects-focused consultation I propose here won't work for all kinds of situations and all kinds of resources. I think it will *often* work, however, and particularly where tribal concerns are involved, people doing Section 106 review should give it a try before opting for the uncreative, time-consuming, expensive, if comfortable and profitable "traditional" way of doing the business of Section 106.

Notes

1. C.f. Fisher, Ury, and Patton 1991.
2. NPS 1983:44720.

Part IV

Thinking about Archeology in CRM

I began my preprofessional (and for that matter, prepubescent) life as a self-identified archeologist, and to this day I find the subject fascinating. Those who study the subject professionally, however, can be another kettle of fish altogether. Archeologists are generally pretty good people individually, but get us in groups and we exhibit some sadly extreme types of herd behavior. Despite our training as anthropologists, which one might think would be broadening, we archeologists are often narrow-minded and chauvinistic, stuck tightly in our own worldviews. Organized in groups (for example, professional societies and committees that write guidelines for practice in the field), we tend to be self-righteous and exclusionary—dogs in the manger who would rather see sites destroyed without study than salvaged by nonprofessionals. Some of us are uncomfortable dealing with living people, especially members of groups who claim descent from, or some other sort of cultural relationship with, the dead folk we study. Almost all of us regard the private ownership of artifacts as a secular version of original sin—while claiming, as a matter of principle, that the artifacts really aren't important at all; it's the information they contain that counts.

Archeologists dominate CRM. Far more archeologists are employed in CRM than are practitioners of history, architectural history, landscape architecture, cultural anthropology, or any other named professional discipline. Most SHPOs and federal agencies hire archeologists to run their

"Section 106 shops," and quite a few Federal Preservation Officers—the top CRM dogs in the federal establishment—are archeologists. In many if not most U.S. academic anthropology departments, CRM is understood to be simply a way of funding archeology.

I continue to call myself an archaeologist, continue to dabble in the field,[1] and am not unhappy about doing either, but I do think that the comfortable, even smug, assurance with which archeologists exercise their assumptions and prejudices in CRM should be questioned from time to time.

Hence the following three chapters. The first is addressed to the employers of CRM practitioners and the readers of reports. It encourages them to be critical in considering what archeologists tell them about CRM and its subject matter. The second was presented to a group of historic preservation educators and deals particularly with the sometimes peculiar ways in which archeologists interpret the "integrity" of historic properties. The third is intended to speak to archeologists, questioning the logic of our ethical standards regarding the private ownership and traffic in artifacts.

Note

1. C.f., King, Jacobson, Burns, and Spading 2001.

18

Archeo-Bias: Recognition and Prevention

A rcheology, often spelled archaeology, is the study of the human past, conducted through the examination of the past's physical leavings. Archeologists typically study "material culture," made up of "artifacts" and other stuff left in and on the ground by people in the past, and "archeological sites"—the places where such stuff was left and can be found. To an archeologist, a "site" is important if it can produce important "data"—that is, information about the past. Sites and "material culture" (architecture, graves, and so forth) are often collectively referred to as "archeological resources."

The United States, like other nations, has laws that deal specifically with archeological resources. Paramount among these is the Archeological Resources Protection Act (ARPA), which in theory prohibits the excavation of archeological resources on public and Indian lands without a permit. ARPA's ancestor, the Antiquities Act of 1906, does essentially the same thing but was found to be "fatally vague" by courts in the 1970s, leading to the enactment of the much tighter, more stringent ARPA. The Archeological and Historic Preservation Act (AHPA) or Archeological Data Preservation Act (ADPA) also passed in the 1970s, requires "data recovery"—that is, the recovery of information through scientific study—from archeological sites threatened by federal, federally assisted, and federally licensed projects. The Abandoned Shipwrecks Act (ASA) deals with a particular kind of archeological site—the submerged sites represented by shipwrecks.

The rest of the nation's cultural resource laws—notably the National Historic Preservation Act—do not deal specifically with archeology as distinguished from other disciplines. Archeological sites are among the resources dealt with by NHPA and some of the other laws, but it is only one such resource among many.

Yet many CRM practitioners, in and out of government, treat NHPA, particularly, as though it were specifically and near-exclusively about archeology—as though it were the National Archeological Preservation Act. Particularly in rural areas, it is not uncommon for surveys ostensibly intended to identify impacts on historic properties (or even all "cultural resources") to give their nearly undivided attention to the identification of archeological sites. Sometimes there are bows to the identification of standing structures; an architectural historian may be hired to perform a "windshield survey"—driving around and looking for old buildings. Sometimes there are bows toward "traditional cultural properties" (TCPs) by somehow consulting (or just sending letters of inquiry to) Indian tribes. Very rarely there is some glimmer of appreciation for cultural landscapes, but usually as something of an afterthought. The core of most rural identification efforts is the conduct of archeological survey, and other resource types are given short shrift.

This sort of thing reflects what I call "archeo-bias"—the practice of narrowly focussing on archeological sites and concerns, to the exclusion of other cultural resources and resource issues.

As an archeologist I can appreciate the reasons for archeo-bias, and as a student of historic preservation's history in the United States I can understand why it exists. But as a cultural resource practitioner I have to deplore it, for several reasons. The most obvious of these is that those who suffer from it tend—unintentionally—to ignore or give insufficient attention to impacts on resources that aren't archeological—that aren't "sites" or don't contain important "data." Archeo-bias can thwart the public's interest—or the interest of specific groups—in addressing project impacts on things of cultural importance that happen not to be archeological sites. Less obviously, archeo-bias can lead people to do things, and fund things, that aren't really required by the law and that aren't very sensible. This can lead to unnecessary project delays and cost overruns. And of course, the flip side of doing things that *aren't* required is that one may very well fail to do things that *are* required, leaving one's agency or client vulnerable to litigation by people who know the law better than the archeologists do.

Consider the case of the Tubular Pipeline, a fictional but reality-based natural gas pipeline from Arkansas to Wyoming.

Tubular requires a certificate from the Federal Energy Regulatory Commission (FERC) before it can be built. The FERC has its own regulations designed to implement NEPA, Section 106, and other environmental protection authorities. These regulations (not very helpfully, and with dubious grounding in the law) require project sponsors, as part of their applications for certificates, to provide a report that includes:

> documentation of initial cultural resource consultation . . . and written comments from SHPOs, THPOs and land-managing agencies. The initial cultural resources consultations should establish the need for surveys. If deemed necessary, the survey report must be filed with the application.[1]

So Tubular's project manager has a meeting with FERC's technical staff, to work out plans for submitting an application for a certificate.

"Looks like we'll have to do a 'survey' if any of the SHPOs or agencies ask us to," the project manager says. "What kind of survey is required?"

FERC's cultural resource specialist—an archeologist—has an easy answer:

"That means a 100 percent pedestrian survey."

"You mean we've got to interview all the pedestrians we run into?"

"No, no, it means you've got to have archeologists walk the entire right-of-way and document all the sites. Then you have to test them to determine if they're eligible for the National Register."

Of course, that's not what FERC's regulations—or the ACHP's Section 106 regulations—say, but lest you think the above is apocryphal, let me tell you that it's almost word for word (well, not the part about interviews) what I was told by a FERC representative the day I began writing this.

What we have here is galloping, metastasizing, archeo-bias. And here's why it's a problem.

First look at it from Tubular's standpoint. There is probably no earthly way they're going to get archeologists to look at every square foot of land along their right-of-way before they need to file their permit application—or if it is possible, it's going to cost them an extraordinary amount of money. And once they've done it, there's every likelihood that somebody's going to pop up later on and say "Hey, what about traditional cultural properties?" Or cultural landscapes, or bridges, or vernacular architecture, or whatever. Whereupon Tubular will find that it's spent its money in vain; it's going to have to fund more work before FERC can finish processing its application.

Now look at it from the standpoint of people who are concerned about cultural resources other than archeological sites. Take, for example, the Passionate Protectors of Putrid Pass (P4) who ascribe great importance to the pristine scenery of a certain pass (with sulfuric geysers) across the Rockies—through which the pipeline is planned to pass. Putrid Pass may well be eligible for the National Register—as a traditional cultural property, as a cultural landscape, or because it's where the Dunder Party died of asphyxiation. But it's not got any archeological sites. And Tubular's surveyors aren't looking at anything but the immediate right-of-way, and aren't concerned about anything other than sites whose data can be messed up by physical impact. So the potential visual impacts of the swath the pipeline will cut through the Putrid Pass landscape isn't considered in the "cultural resource survey report" that Tubular's consultants complete. If P4 is politically astute, has the money to hire a good lawyer, is good at making noise, maybe they can get it considered—to Tubular's considerable cost as well as their own—but what if they're not any of these things? What if P4 is a tiny little Indian tribe, maybe one that's not Federally recognized? An impoverished rural Hispanic community? A group of antigovernment isolationists? Chances are that they'll simply be deprived of the opportunity to have their concerns addressed in planning the pipeline or in FERC's regulatory process.

Archeo-bias is pretty easy to recognize. It's typically reflected in:

- A tendency to use the word "site" a lot, often as a synonym for "historic property."

- Use of the term "cultural resource," usually without definition but actually meaning archeological site or maybe not-yet-evaluated possible historic property.

- Employing or requiring the employment only of archeologists to carry out CRM tasks.

- A tendency to equate a project's area of potential effects (APE) with the area in which physical ground disturbance will take place.

- Emphasis on the conduct of "pedestrian surveys."

- A tendency to "write off" areas that have been "disturbed."

- Belief in the employment of standard survey methods, usually designated things like "Phase I," "Class II," and so on.

- Equation of background research with checking SHPO or other "site files."

- Little attention to consultation with interested groups, with the possible and often rather superficial exception of Indian tribes.

- Considering the significance of properties largely with reference to their information content—if they may contain interesting data they're significant; if they probably don't, they aren't.

- A perception that if a property can be physically avoided by a project (sometimes called "preservation in place" or simply "avoidance"), the project will automatically have no impact on the property.

- Equation of "mitigation" with "data recovery"—i.e., excavation.

So, how do you avoid being victimized by archeo-bias—whether you're concerned about proper consideration of resources and impacts or whether you're concerned about getting timely, cost-effective, and relatively bullet-proof Section 106 review done on your project? There are several strategies; which ones you can employ depends on who you are, what the project is, how it's brought into review under the CRM laws (as a direct federal action, via a regulatory agency, etc.) and where you are in the process. Here are some suggestions:

- If you're planning a project that requires review, or representing someone who is:
  1. Don't just hire an archeologist to take care of your problems.

Even if you're fairly sure (for some reason) that all your problems will be with archeological sites, it's a good idea to look for a firm or individual with some professional breadth and depth, so that if unexpected problems with historical architecture, landscapes, traditional cultural properties, roads and trails, or whatever come up, the contractor is at least prepared to recognize that they exist.

2. Prepare a thoughtful scope of work for identification. Base this on scoping consultation and background research. Ask yourself and others what's already known about the area—its history, its ethnography, its architecture. Look the area over; are there a bunch of old buildings? A nice rural landscape? Pristine natural areas? Is there a Native American group or other community anywhere in the vicinity that's likely to have ties to the land? Use your answers to these questions, based on your observations and consultation, to prepare your scope of work. Do *not* automatically accept somebody's insistence (whether it's an SHPO, a THPO, a regulatory agency specialist, or your consultant) that a Class XYZ survey, whatever that is, is both required and sufficient to your needs.

3. Pay attention to what your contractor is doing; make sure he's not putting all his effort into archeology and failing to consult local people, look for non-archeological historic properties, consider other-than-direct-physical effects.

4. Challenge your contractor. One of the dumbest things you can do is say "Well, he's the expert, not me, so I'll just do what he says." He may be an expert in archeology, but that doesn't make him an expert in Section 106, in historic preservation, in CRM. None of which are much like rocket science; there's nothing in them that a lay person can't understand. You may not like what you come to understand, but it doesn't need to be a mystery.

• If you're an outside reviewer of a project or program, perhaps an opponent of a project, the presence of archeo-bias may give you a very easy opportunity to be critical, even to bring review to a halt while better data are acquired.

1. Be on the lookout for the signs of archeo-bias described above. When you see them, look at what the implications of their presence are. Has archeo-bias caused a failure to consider the interests of affected communities? Has it caused everything to focus on direct physical impacts to the exclusion of less direct, less physical effects? Articulate these problems in your review.

2. Educate yourself about what the law and regulations really require. Don't trust the archeologists to interpret them for you.

3. Ask embarrassing questions. "How did you address impacts on cultural landscapes during your Class III.B(5) survey?" Don't be discouraged by your certainty that the answer will be thoroughly inadequate. Learn to enjoy putting damn fool archeologists (and their employers) on the spot.

And if you're an archeologist, be of good cheer; archeo-bias can be cured. Rigorously review your own writing, and your own thinking, for evidence of archeo-bias, and try to weed it out. If you run a consulting firm, make sure you have access to all the necessary expertise to address your clients' cultural resource needs, not just the archeology that you're interested in. Think through the scopes of work that you help write, and question those you may receive, to make sure they're not archeo-biased. You may not be a better person for all this, but you'll be a better participant in cultural resource management. Like it or not, CRM isn't just applied archeology.

Note

1. 18 CFR 380.12(f)(2); see also 18 CFR 380.14.

19

*Integrity among Archeologists: The Dirty Truth**

A few years ago, shortly after my fiftieth birthday, Druscilla Null of the Advisory Council on Historic Preservation and I were teaching a course in Alaska. I mentioned that I had recently become sufficiently antique to qualify as an historic property, if only I were a piece of real estate. Dru kindly put her arm around my shoulders and said:

"No, Tom; you have no integrity."[1]

Fair enough, and a comment that probably applies to lots of us archeologists. On many levels (as it were), integrity is not something we think much about. Or more accurately perhaps, we think about it in somewhat limited ways that differ from the way many other preservation practitioners conceptualize it.

Some of the parameters along which preservationists usually measure integrity have little relevance to archeologists or to archeological sites as appraised by archeologists. "Workmanship," for example, doesn't mean much to us in most cases. I'm not even sure what "integrity of workmanship" would mean in an archeological context. That the artifacts represent pure styles? Lacking purity wouldn't necessarily disqualify a building; why

---

*Presented to the "Multiple Views, Multiple Meanings" Conference, National Council for Preservation Education, Gaucher College, March 12, 1999.

should it disqualify an archeological site? "Design" and "materials" are similar head-scratchers for archeologists.

And then there's "feeling." It's safe to assume that archeological sites don't feel anything, but then, we can assume the same of buildings. Archeologists develop feelings for the sites they dig, but the fact that I really *felt good* about the Schwabacher Site on the Chowchilla River in California wasn't something I'd mention in a National Register nomination to impress the Keeper. And the fact that the site of Iras Village in Micronesia had been covered by an airport, and hence didn't *feel* anything like an old Chuukese village, didn't make it any less eligible for the Register. No, "integrity of feeling" doesn't mean much from an archeological perspective.

"Integrity of association" is sensible—if the site isn't associated with something important, it logically can't be eligible. But how does something *lose* integrity of association? By being picked up and moved away? Perhaps, but from an archeological point of view, a Clovis site that's been scraped up by belly loaders and deposited somewhere else hasn't lost its *association* with Clovis; it's lost its integrity of *location* and *setting*. These two parameters have pretty clear meaning to archeologists; "association" is a lot more slippery.

But really, the main integrity measure for archeologists isn't even mentioned explicitly in the National Register's list though it's implicit in most: integrity of *condition*. What kind of shape is the place in?

In essence, for an archeologist, a site has integrity if it is in a physical condition that permits study of the data it contains. Nothing else really matters.

Archeologists can be *very* narrow-minded about this kind of thing and have a lot of trouble understanding that there is any *other* possible measure of integrity. To the descendant of some ancient community, the feeling conveyed by that community's village site—or the place where the community left nothing at all for archeologists to study, but that's associated with an important tradition—can be extremely important. Losing integrity of feeling may effectively destroy the place in the eyes of such a person, even if no physical disruption occurs at all. To the same person, total physical disruption may be irrelevant, if somehow integrity of feeling is retained. To someone interested in developing a site for public interpretive purposes, feeling and association may also be critical factors, regardless of the physical condition of the site. Archeologists often have

a hard time getting their arms around non-research-based aspects of significance, and therefore around non-research-based measures of integrity.
This causes a number of problems for our nonarcheological colleagues in
preservation and for the public.

To develop these points a bit, I want to look at two of the questions
that have been put before us by the conference organizers: "How much
can a place change and retain its integrity?" and "Who defines integrity?"

Change and Integrity

Since the significance of an archeological site to an archeologist depends
on its capacity to produce useful research data, the amount and kind of integrity a site must have depends on the kind of research questions one is
asking. Some of these questions, and the data they require, can seem pretty
strange to nonarcheologists, and some really *are* pretty questionable. But
there may be good reasons to find out, say, whether makers of Hoitytoity
Black-on-Puce pottery plied their trade in the Rushing River Valley. If
that's all we need to know—did they or did they not make that kind of
pottery in that valley—then it doesn't much matter if all the ancient village sites along the River have been churned up by repeated plowing or
the construction of wall-to-wall Wal-Marts. If we can dig 'em up and see
if there are Hoitytoity sherds in them, they have integrity vis-à-vis that
particular research question. On the other hand, if answering some important research question requires precise data on the spatial organization
of Hoitytoity pottery factories, disturbance of the sites is going to be a really serious problem.

Research interests change through time and are pretty individualistic.
Fifty years ago, archeologists were mostly interested in reconstructing
"culture history." Such history was best reconstructed, it was thought, by
studying deep, stratified sites. Ergo, these were the kinds of sites that were
valued, and if a site's stratigraphy had been mucked up, it had lost integrity. Then what were called "Settlement Archeology" and "New Archeology" burst on the scene, with interests in a wide range of cultural
processes that could be investigated by looking at a lot of different kinds
of archeological phenomena. Suddenly little, unstratified sites became important for what they could tell us about settlement patterns or seasonal
rounds, and stratigraphy became only an aspect of a site's structure that

might or might not be useful to research. Today there are many kinds of archeologists, pursuing many different kinds of research. The data that are important to one kind are not necessarily important to another, so the fact that a given body of data has been destroyed may be a lot more important to one archeologist than to another. An archeologist who's interested in gender studies may find little left to interest her in a site that's been reduced to flaked stone tools on the surface of the desert, but an archeologist who specializes in lithic technology may regard the same site as a prime candidate for research.

So the archeological answer to the question: "How much can a place change and retain its integrity" is, "It depends." It depends on the research questions one is interested in. It depends on the thinking of the person formulating the research questions. It can be the subject of endless argument. It can change through time. The site that's regarded as lacking integrity today may gain it tomorrow, if a new research question comes along that is less—or differently—demanding of spatial integrity than those considered before. There simply are no hard-and-fast rules.

And there can't be—*mustn't be.* Archeology is, after all, supposed to be a science of sorts, and in every science, what's important to observe and measure can and almost invariably does change through time. This is in the nature of science, and it's fruitless to look for certainty. What constitutes archeological integrity is the product of current thinking about archeological research.

For this reason, the commonly used rule of thumb that a place should be recognizable to those who made it, or used it during its period of significance, doesn't hold up with archeological sites. Archie Archaic, who lived 3,000 years ago at the junction of the Monongahela, the Allegheny, and the Ohio, almost certainly wouldn't recognize his old home town in modern-day Pittsburgh, but that wouldn't make the place ineligible for the Register. It would have integrity from an archeological perspective if we could learn something useful from it about Archie and his society.

It may be worth mentioning again that what archeologists may find useful to learn from something like Archie's homesite may seem pretty strange to nonarcheologists. Learning that Archie and his family lived as a single family rather than as part of a large, settled community, for example, may not seem like a very big deal to nonarcheologists, but when put together with comparative data from many other sites it may actually have profound implications for studies of social evolution, environmental change, and a host of other large issues.

Who Defines Integrity?

Largely because we think we can learn important things from very humble and often esoteric things, it's an article of faith among archeologists that archeologists are the only ones who can judge archeological significance. What looks like a pile of junk, or an empty field, or a parking lot to the untrained eye may be accurately identified by an archeologist as a source of tremendously important archeological data. But the narrow-mindedness with which archeologists often make judgments about significance and integrity can make this a dangerous notion to adopt too literally. The danger is compounded by the fact that in most SHPO offices and in many federal agencies, archeologists are the dominant parties in the conduct of Section 106 review, so they're called upon to evaluate not only archeological sites but all kinds of other historic properties as well.

Let's look at these points in a little detail.

Recognizing Integrity

Over the last thirty years or so, there's been a growing interest among archeologists in what are called "transformation processes"—the processes by which a living community's leavings get translated into what we read as the archeological record. Transformation processes are not simple affairs. They're influenced by a tremendous range of natural and cultural factors. What are the leavings made of? How quickly do they decompose? What's the climate like and what does it do to the rate of decomposition? What about soil conditions? Are there animals that carry stuff around? Do later people scavenge for stuff? Is there erosion? Deposition? Later construction? Plowing? An archeologist looking at a site to judge its integrity has to juggle all these kinds of factors, because transformation is what integrity of condition is all about. A site that has been totally transformed isn't there anymore; it has completely returned to Mother Earth. But there are a lot of stops along the way, and there's no single way that transformation happens. It's a complex business, and being wrong can have serious consequences.

At the famous African Burial Ground (ABG) in New York City, although old maps indicated the existence of the cemetery in the eighteenth century, nineteenth-century maps showed that the site had been built over, and the nineteenth-century buildings had had basements. So when the maps were found during environmental impact analysis for a new federal building planned on the site, it was assumed that the cemetery had been pretty much transformed out of existence—churned up by basement digging into a meaningless (to archeologists) mélange of bones. But one crucial transformatitive factor wasn't considered: nobody looked at how the surface of the ground had changed between the time the Burial Ground was in use and the time the buildings were built. It turned out that the Burial Ground had been in a low place, and it had been filled over, so many, many burials were intact under the basements, which had penetrated only the fill. That mistake—combined with several others—cost the General Services Administration (GSA) tens of millions of dollars.

So judging the integrity of a site for archeological research really *is* a job for an archeologist—somebody with some training in transformation processes, who thinks about such things. But nonarcheologists should note that the basis for making such judgments is something that the archeologist should be able to explain to a nonarcheologist, and something the nonarcheologist shouldn't be shy about questioning. It should have taken neither a rocket scientist nor an archeologist to have thought about the possibility of overfilling at the ABG site, and you'd think that some smart civil engineer would have raised a question about it. But nobody did, and that was a mistake.

Which brings us to the second point.

Archeological Blinders

Failure to recognize how the African Burial Ground had been (and hadn't been) transformed through time was one of the things that ended up costing GSA vast amounts of money, time, and embarrassment. The bigger problem was failure to recognize it as having significance that went *beyond* archeological research. Viewing the site as something "the archeologists will take care of," GSA moved forward with advanced planning, building demolition, and site preparation. The contractor was mobilized to begin construction by the time excavations began to show that there were lots and lots more quite intact dead people in the ground there than anyone had anticipated. Word got out to the African American community that GSA was about to start violating the remains of the ancestors, and the results were worthy of the fact that the site literally opened on Broadway. Demonstrations, a congressional investigation, work stoppage, redesign, millions lost in penalties paid to the contractor—on and on. This all happened largely because GSA had not sat down with the community in advance and talked about the matter. In a comparative study of the ABG and the African Baptist Church cemetery excavation in Philadelphia, John McCarthy has shown clearly how working with the community in the latter case avoided the kind of expensive confrontation that happened in the former.[2]

You're obviously not going to talk to a community about its ancestral sites if you don't think about the community's possible interests in them—if it doesn't occur to you that these interests could be important. Archeologists are not always very good about doing this kind of thing. Nor are we very good about recognizing the interests of nonarcheological preservation practitioners, nor about recognizing the factors that give or don't give a place significance and integrity from another discipline's point of view.

A few years ago, while working on a military base closure, I read a newspaper article on the subject. It quoted the closing agency's "cultural resources manager," who of course was an archeologist, as saying that the base was really important because of what we could learn from its buildings about early twentieth-century military industrial processes. In point of fact, there was probably very little the base could teach us about such processes, and still less that anybody really needed to know. What was important about the base had nothing to do with research; it had to do with the ambience of the place, the kinds of architectural styles and engineering processes its buildings and structures represented, its historical connections with the community, and its potential for adaptive use. But all the archeologist could talk about was research potential, because that was the only kind of significance he had been trained to consider. So, had the base lost its ability to teach us something that an archeologist could see as important, the archeologist would have judged that it had lost integrity, even though its ambience (that is, its "feeling") and associations were perfectly intact and its reuse potential unimpaired.

In the case of the African Burial Ground, we'll never know how messed up the site would have to have been before it lost its significance in the eyes of the descendent community, but it's safe to guess that it would have retained this significance long after it had lost its archeological research value. If it had been all churned up by the nineteenth-century basements, it would have retained little importance for archeological research, but it's safe to say that the descendent community would still have been unhappy to see the ancestors' bones being poured into dump trucks for a ride to the local landfill. And assuring them that the site had lost its integrity as a subject of scientific study would probably have had little mollifying effect.

You've got to watch archeologists very carefully about things like this. Not long ago I heard an agency archeologist talking about a landscape to which an Indian tribe ascribed cultural and religious significance. His agency had sponsored a major ethnographic study, which had documented the significance of the place in the eyes of the tribe.

"We'll be initiating Section 106 review of impacts on the area," he said, "as soon as we can get our archeologists out to look at it and verify its integrity."

What, he was asked, did he expect his archeologists to find? Sherds of significance? Flakes of feeling? If the place retained significance in the eyes of those whose cultural traditions made it significance, what useful observations could an archeologist add? He had no answer—just looked vaguely befuddled by the question.

Conclusion

So the bottom line is this:

1. Integrity to an archeologist means that a place is not so mucked up that it can't yield useful research data.

2. How much mucking up this takes depends on the research questions one asks.

3. The questions one asks vary with the scholar's research interests, and change through time.

4. Archeologists tend to have trouble thinking about significance—and hence about integrity—in terms other than those related to data content.

So you never ought to trust an archeologist with judging integrity in any context other than that of research potential, and even in that context you need to recognize that there are no absolutes. The integrity of an archeological site is largely if not entirely in the eye of the beholder.

So if you can't trust an archeologist to judge the integrity of an archeological site, who are you gonna call? And what can we do about the fact that, like it or not, archeologists *do* mostly run the Section 106 compliance shops around the country?

I think the only answers to these questions lie in a lot more cross-training and truly interdisciplinary training both for current practitioners and for students heading into the preservation work force. Preservationists of all flavors need to understand that there are multiple ways to judge significance and integrity. We *all* need to be moderately conversant with *all* approaches, and we need to be smart enough to know when we're getting out of our depth—when to call in a specialist. And we need to be smart enough to ask the specialist intelligent questions, challenge his or her biases, rather than just "leaving it to the archeologists" or the architectural historians, or landscape historians, or whoever.

Ultimately, I think we need practitioners who don't think of themselves as archeologists or architectural historians or landscape historians, but as interdisciplinary preservation experts, or cultural resource managers, or something of the kind. And who not only think of themselves as such, and call themselves that, but who have a breadth of knowledge to match.

One last suggestion. I've talked a lot about the mutability of archeological judgment—that what's got integrity today may not tomorrow, and vice versa, depending on what we see as important research questions, or important bodies of data for pursuing such questions. I really think the same principle applies more broadly, though admittedly in somewhat different ways. I suppose there are some things that are always going to be significant, or are always not going to be, but I think there's a very large class of properties out there that sort of slosh back and forth.

I had a call the other day from a potential client—he decided not to be, once we talked—who wanted help proving that a farmstead that was in the way of his development project wasn't eligible for the National Register. "It's just like my grandma's farm," he fumed. I explained that his grandma's farm might very well be eligible, too. "Then what's *not* eligible?" he asked. "Weeelllll . . ." I said.

The farmstead that troubled my erstwhile client was judged eligible because someone had occasion to do so (the occasion being a Section 106 review of his project), and because someone (its owners) cared enough to press the issue. Another identical farmstead, under different circumstances, would not be judged eligible, or might even explicitly be judged ineligible.

This sort of ambiguity is perfectly normal and expectable in the real world—my own opinions of things change through time, my opinions are not the same as your opinions, and how much either of us values something may vary with the conditions under which we evaluate it. That's life, that's reality. But it's not the National Register, which is based on the notion that things either are or are not significant, now and forevermore. Really a rather quaint notion. As we go into a new millennium, I wonder if the time hasn't come to grow beyond it.[3]

Notes

1. For historic places, however, "integrity" is a wholly amoral concept. The National Register regulations, at 36 CFR 60.4, say that to be eligible for the Register, a property must have "integrity of location, design, setting, materials, workmanship, feeling, and association."

2. McCarthy 1996.

3. For further treatment of this subject, see King 1998:73–101; 244–47.

20

A 1937 Winged Liberty Head Dime from Silver Spring, Maryland

In 1986, when my wife and I achieved the American Dream and bought a house in the suburbs, we undertook some landscaping in the backyard. The work required excavating an area about 12 by 2.5 m, oriented NE–SW, to a depth of between 30 and 60 cm. Believing that some twenty-five years in archaeology had surely taught me something, I did the shovel work myself and screened the excavated soil.

The results of the excavation were on the whole negative—a few tools attributable to the previous residents' do-it-yourself auto repairs, some construction debris, and a modest assemblage of "G.I. Joe" plastic weaponry, circa 1986, confidently identified by its seven-year-old owner as intrusive.

However, I did find a dime.

The dime, located in the upper 10 cm of the south-central portion of the excavation, was a Winged Liberty Head or "Mercury" type, designed by Adolph A. Weinman, dated 1937, and minted in Philadelphia, Pennsylvania.

Having examined the dime carefully, and recorded the above information about it, I took it to Bonanza Coin and Stamp in downtown Silver Spring, Maryland, and sold it for thirty-eight cents ($0.38). We added these proceeds to my wife's annual contribution to the Archaeological Conservancy.

My action in selling the dime raises a fundamental question about my ethics as a properly degreed and, certified archeologist—to wit, do I have any?

Calvin Cummings[1] has conveniently summarized the ethical standards of the nation's various archaeological societies regarding the selling of artifacts. Review of Cummings's paper indicates the following:

The Society for American Archaeology (SAA), of which I am a member, pledges itself in its bylaws to "discourage commercialism in the archaeological field and to work for its elimination." It goes on to declare that "selling archaeological materials for the sole purpose of personal satisfaction or financial gain" is "contrary to the ideals and objects of the Society."

The Society of Professional Archaeologists (SOPA), of which I am a founding member and which certified me to be a professional, declares in its "Canons of Professionalism" that a professional archaeologist has the responsibility to "[d]iscourage, and if possible prevent, destruction of archaeological sites, or portions of sites for the purpose of acquiring materials for other than scientific purposes."

The Society for California Archaeology (SCA), which lacks jurisdiction in Maryland but to whose views I, as a founding member and one-time president, should attend, flatly declares in its by-laws that the "gathering of archaeological specimens . . . for purposes of selling artifacts . . . shall in all instances be forbidden."

The Society for Historical Archaeology (SHA), which does not count me among its members but whose views on the subject would seem to be relevant given the chronological context of my excavation, declares in its by-laws that the "selling of archaeological artifacts . . . for the purpose of personal satisfaction or financial gain . . . [is] . . . contrary to the purposes of the Society."

The SHA takes these strictures so seriously that it denies its members the opportunity to share the scholarly results of their work with their peers at Society meetings if that work has been sponsored by someone who intends to sell all or some of the resulting artifacts.[2]

By selling the dime I found I surely violated all the above ethical standards; yet I feel no guilt. The question I pose to the reader is: Should I feel guilt? If not, why not, and what does my absence of guilt say about the ethical codes cited above?

One reason not to feel guilt might be that because of its age, my dime was not an "archaeological artifact." There is some statutory basis for this excuse: The Archaeological Resources Protection Act (ARPA) defines an "archaeological resource" as including only "material remains of past human life or activities" which are "at least 100 years of age."[3] I am uncomfortable with this excuse. Historical archeologists regularly and correctly complain about the "100-year rule." William Rathje and his colleagues have brilliantly demonstrated the applicability of archaeology to quite contemporary phenomena,[4] and there is growing scholarly interest in the archaeology of such recent historical events as World War II.

Clearly there must be temporal limits on an archeologist's exercise of ethical responsibility toward the care of artifacts, or we would be unable to take out yesterday's trash. But one hundred years is far too distant a limit. If we accept fifty years as a threshold of antiquity, following the criteria of the National Register of Historic Places,[5] then my dime was old enough to qualify as a possible archaeological resource. If we deny the usefulness of arbitrary age limits in general, as I believe is preferable, then chronology by itself gives my guilt no assuagement.

Perhaps I am guiltless because the dime was not found in an archaeological site? But what is an archaeological site? In the distant undergraduate days when I had to ponder this question, a site was defined either as the locus of past human activity that had left some remains amenable to study, or as the locus of an archeologist's excavation. By either definition my homesite qualifies. People have lived there for several decades at least, and it was obviously the location of my excavation. True, it is not listed in Maryland's archaeological inventory, but many perfectly good archaeological sites, historic and prehistoric, share that distinction. True, it didn't produce much of an artifact assemblage, but as a colleague of my youth correctly used to put it, "negative data are positive data." More significantly, in recent years we as a profession have come more and more to recognize the research utility of "isolated occurrences" and the importance of addressing "nonsite archaeology."[6] So it doesn't really matter whether the dime was in a site or not. It was at least an isolated occurrence, used by someone in the past, which I dug up and sold.

Of course I donated the proceeds to a worthy cause that advances the purposes of archaeology, so arguably I did not sell the dime "for the sole purpose of personal satisfaction or financial gain."[7] The "purpose" caveat in the SAA and SHA by-laws raises some intriguing possibilities, but in terms of the way our professional ethics are commonly interpreted it hardly seems material. If the plunderer of a Mayan tomb sold its contents and donated the proceeds to the SAA, it would doubtless raise eyebrows. The fact that a heroin merchant uses his gains to support a home for abused urchins makes those gains no less ill-gotten. The fact that these examples involve substantial amounts of money while my dime only brought in thirty-eight cents also seems to me irrelevant; to paraphrase the old joke, we've established what sort of archeologist I am; we're just haggling about the price.

Perhaps I feel no guilt because I take the dime, like my daily garbage, to have no research significance. After all, what can we learn from the fact that sometime during or after 1937, someone discarded, hid, or lost a dime in the backyard of a home in Silver Spring? The fact tells us nothing of importance about the past; ergo, my disposal of the dime is of no archaeological concern.

But was the dime really worthless for research? What if next year or in the next decade someone develops a technique for determining, from the surface chemistry of a coin, the age, economic status, sexual preferences, and political affiliations of its last three users? Won't it be unfortunate, and reprehensible, that I failed to retain a source of such data for analysis?

Obviously in deciding to sell the dime I made a judgment—judging that nobody is likely to come up with a technique that will allow us to elicit much data from an isolated 1937 coin, and that even if someone did, the data we would thus be able to glean would probably be trivial.

Allowing me to make and act on such a judgment leads us onto some rather shaky ground. Where do we draw the line on the legitimacy of such judgments? What if the dime had been dated 1837 rather than 1937? What if there had been five together instead of one in isolation? What if it had been a 1537 doubloon? A Clovis Point? A retouched flake? A Hohokam potsherd? Three Hohokam potsherds?

There might be a high level of agreement among archeologists that I would I not be justified in selling, say, a Clovis Point found in my backyard. I suspect, however, that reasonable people could differ about one or more 1837 coins, an isolated flake, a doubloon, or a few potsherds of Arizona origin in the disturbed backyard deposit of a twentieth-century residence in Maryland. If this is true, then can reasonable—even ethical—people not differ about, say, the cargo of a treasure ship or the contents of a bottle dump? Is a chest full of doubloons, or a cargo of silver ingots scattered on the seabed, likely to yield data of sufficient import to justify retaining it forever in a curatorial institution? Assuming we can recover the stuff using proper techniques, and can weigh, measure, photograph and fondle every coin or bar before it is sold, have we really lost significant data and behaved unethically if we sell it? What about 400 identical Vaseline jars from the privy pits of a nineteenth-century house of ill repute? How about two complete Anasazi pots from a site that produces fifty thousand sherds representing similar vessels? If we save the sherds but sell the pots after their full recordation, have we discarded data? What data? If I can legitimately judge that the dime I found is of little enough research significance that it need not be preserved for future use, and if I can act on that judgment without scandalizing my comrades-in-ethics, then surely I can make and act on similar judgments about doubloons, ingots, Vaseline jars, and Anasazi pots. If not, why not?

I have led the reader through this lengthy exposition to suggest that we behave illogically when we adopt rigid ethical strictures against things like the sale of artifacts. I suggest that the question of what it is and is not legitimate for an archeologist or the sponsor of an archaeological project to sell would benefit more from dispassionate analysis than from the adoption and enforcement of rigid ethical codes. I suggest that we try to establish by consensus a system for distinguishing between those artifacts whose long-range research potential demands their permanent curation and those that most likely lack such potential, and then seek curation of the former[8] but readily accept, even encourage, traffic in the latter, provided they are obtained in ways that do not destroy significant data or outrage descendent communities. If we could reach and act on such consensus, we might be able to create a rational legal system to protect archaeological sites and data, discouraging pothunting on lands both public and private while satisfying the market forces, esthetic values, and plain curiosity that make pothunting a growth industry today. We might be able to strike up some mutually beneficial partnerships with treasure salvors, art dealers and collectors who today go about their businesses in blissful ignorance of, or perhaps with amusement for, such hand-wringing exercises in ethical etheria as the SHA's decision not to allow archeologists employed by salvors to present papers at its annual meeting. We might even generate contributions of more than thirty-eight cents to such worthy causes as the Archaeological Conservancy.

Responsible replies are welcome, as are volunteers for my next back-yard excavation.

Notes

I am grateful to John M. Fowler, Esq., Deputy Executive Director of the Advisory Council on Historic Preservation and purveyor of antiques, for technical advice in preparation of this chapter.

1. Cummings 1983.
2. C.f., Hamilton 1988.
3. ARPA 1979 Sec. 3(1).
4. C.f., Rathje and Murphy 2001.
5. NPS 1981: 36 CFR 60.4.
6. C.f., Thomas 1975.
7. C.f., SAA by-laws.
8. Where other legitimate public interests, for example the need to repatriate or rebury human remains and grave goods, do not render curation inappropriate.

Conclusion: Lafayette, Where Are You? The European Union, Cultural Heritage, and CRM in the United States

Introduction: Starting Over

In accepting my proposal for this book, which at the time we called "The Book of Tracts," AltaMira Press's Mitch Allen insisted that I write a concluding chapter that he called "If I Were King." This chapter, he said, should tell readers how I would organize the U.S. cultural resource management program if I had the authority to do so, based on my thirty-five years of curmudgeonly experience.

Fair enough. It's easy and fun to criticize, but if I think that the current U.S. CRM system stinks, I should be able to tell people what I think a good system would look like.

But I found the chapter difficult to write, largely because it seemed a fruitless enterprise. I don't have the authority to change the U.S. system, and those who do have scant interest in reform and even less in my thoughts on the subject.

My writing began to gain traction when I thought about the matter hypothetically—how I might, if the opportunity arose, start afresh with another country. But I soon found that such real-world candidates as Afghanistan present real-world challenges too complex to be addressed without a whole lot of study, and when I tried to hypothesize a CRM system for Atlantis or Middle-Earth, I found myself lapsing into silliness.

Then I stumbled upon the fact—well known, I'm sure, to everyone but us provincials—that there actually *is* a "new nation" of a sort that's developing policy and legislation to guide CRM. The European Union (EU) calls it "cultural heritage," but it comes to the same thing. Maybe the EU could reflect upon our experience in the United States and devise a better way of dealing with cultural resources, whatever one calls them.

The EU? I'm suggesting *Europe* as a place for experimentation with new approaches to cultural resources? Well, yes. Certainly neither the EU's constituent nations nor their national cultural heritage systems are new; each has its own history, its own institutions, its own beliefs about what cultural heritage is and how it ought to be managed. But the EU *itself* is new, and the very fact that there is such a plethora of national-level heritage programs among its member nations means that the EU cannot adopt an existing model without infuriating or being ignored by those loyal to others. The EU must look afresh at how to manage cultural heritage and the things that affect it. Furthermore, there is so much angst across the continent about what the EU will do to national and regional identities that the Union has even more reason than the United States to be sensitive to cultural differences. I doubt if Indian tribes have anything on Tuscan pasta makers and Bordeaux vintners for fierceness in their attachment to tradition. The EU is certainly going to have to struggle with cultural heritage policy—already is struggling with it—and maybe some suggestions from across the sea would not be entirely unwelcome.

What Should the EU Do?

So, with some trepidation, since nobody (other than Mitch) has asked me and I've never been east of Dover, here are some suggestions to the EU.

Recommendation 1: Define "cultural heritage" broadly. UNESCO has already done this on Europe's behalf, defining "culture" as "all distinctive, spiritual and material intellectual and emotional features which characterize a society or a social group."[1] That's a good definition to work with; don't narrow it. Don't make the mistake of thinking only about physical things— buildings, sites, objects, monuments and designated historic areas. Physical things have no intrinsic significance. We *assign*

171

significance to such things, based on our beliefs, our values, our feelings. These intangible "things" are the real cultural heritage; they, and the things that affect them, are what Europe needs to manage. Yes, archeologists, of course one of the things Europeans hold dear is knowledge, including knowledge about the past. Yes, architectural historians, Europeans also cherish their cathedrals and castles, farmsteads and villages. Let's stipulate all that, but let's also recognize that there are lots of other things that Europeans—like all other humans—hold dear. Traditions, folkways, dance forms; vistas, sounds, smells; stories, pictures, ways of talking; the experience of mystery; spiritual power; the memory of ancestors. And let's always remember that the cultural value of physical places is in the end itself a cluster of cognitive constructs.

Recommendation 2: Be very skeptical of the notion that cultural significance is forever. Values *do* change over time. Perhaps people thought that community sheep-shearing was really important five years ago, but now that it's gone defunct, interest has shifted to community dance contests as a means of maintaining cultural integrity. That's OK; that's human; that's life.

Recommendation 3: Don't create a formal, official register of valued cultural heritage. Sure, it may be useful to keep track of some of them, to record and map those that hold still, and to whose management such documentation is relevant, but don't get hung up on listing things or not listing them, or give credence only to things that qualify for a list—whether it's the EU's list or the schedule maintained by a member nation. Be concerned about what's important to people, regardless of whether some official says it meets his or her criteria for registration. And the fact that something isn't amenable to listing or putting on a map shouldn't bar it from being considered in planning. If people value lemming watching, then government planners should be careful about doing things that may affect lemming behavior, regardless of whether such behavior can be mapped, or lemmings prevailed upon to be registered. List, if you must, those things in which someone is willing to invest money or some other valuable commodity in preserving—parks, monuments, that kind of thing—but don't make the mistake the United States has made with its National Register, using it as the sole and universal tool for representing significance. Listing is useful for some kinds of heritage resources, but for most, it's pointless, and even where it's relevant it can be deeply misleading.

Recommendation 4: Don't base the EU heritage system on the notion of preserving the past, or contemporary culture, unchanged. Whether one likes it or not, even Gibraltar changes with time and weather. Change happens, and a public policy based on the notion that it's desirable to keep it from happening is doomed to failure and frustration. Change is not bad. It's not necessarily good, either, it just *is*.

Recommendation 5: But *do* recognize, explicitly and with humility, that in every change there's both gain and loss. Europeans—including those involved in government and economic development—should agree among themselves that each European's sense of gain and loss must be respected. Not just each government, or each properly legislated authority, or even each ethnic group, but each individual European. Thus it ought to be policy to try to minimize the sense of loss that each European feels as a result of change—while understanding that this does not mean that change can or should be kept from occurring and that respecting someone's feelings does not necessarily mean acquiescing in their wishes.

Recommendation 6: Recognizing that change is inevitable and necessary, and that change hurts, establish a system for resolving conflicts over cultural heritage issues. It will come as no surprise to readers of this volume's other essays that I suggest this system as the core of the EU's approach to cultural heritage.

Recommendation 7: The conflict resolution system should not focus on resolving issues of "what's significant," and it particularly shouldn't try to resolve such issues through recourse to some high government authority. The national governments of Europe have such systems, God knows, that have developed

over scores of generations, complete with elaborate procedures and substantial bureaucracies. Leave them alone; they're
cultural resources in their own right. Focus on resolving conflicts between change and whatever people think is important
to them—people in communities as well as in positions of
governmental or academic authority. If someone thinks some
bit of culture is important—whether that someone is a
national cultural ministry or a tiny community somewhere in
the Pyrenees—that belief ought to be respected, with the
clear understanding that giving respect is not the same as giving the power of veto. Having established that someone values something for cultural reasons, and that some impending
change may destroy or diminish that something, the cultural
heritage system should focus on resolving that conflict, understanding that "resolution" may mean anything from full
preservation of the valued bit of culture to its unmitigated
loss, and from going ahead with the proposed change to for-
going it altogether. Usually, of course, resolution will mean
something that falls in the midrange between such poles.

Recommendation 8: Recognize the simple, intuitively obvious, but
often forgotten principle that—as we colorful ex-colonials
say—there's more than one way to skin a cat. There are lots
and lots of ways to manage the various aspects of Europe's cultural environment, and to deal with the effects of change. No
one way is necessarily better than another. Different strategies
make sense in different circumstances, and with different
kinds of resources. Let flexibility be the watchword.

Recommendation 9: Make broad-based consultation with all
stakeholders the heart of the conflict resolution system. Define "stakeholders" liberally; give everyone a seat at the negotiating table. Mandate the use of informed, principled negotiation[2] among all concerned parties, leading where possible
to written agreements about how impacts will be mitigated or
at least managed.

So, the kind of cultural heritage system I'd recommend to the EU, if
asked, is one that seeks—through reasoning together by all relevant par-

ties—to manage change in a way that maximizes its benefits to society both in general and in particular groups and settings, while minimizing the destruction of what Europeans—writ large or small—hold dear. And I stress again that what Europeans hold dear isn't just old buildings and sites, streetscapes and neighborhoods and landscapes. It's feelings, beliefs, values, which may or may not involve physical places.

It turns out that the EU has a policy basis for building such a system. Culture—in general, not just buildings and such—is explicitly identified in the Treaty of Maastricht, the EU's organic legislation, and the Union commits itself there to make sure it's considered in planning:

> The Community (sic: the EU) shall take cultural aspects into account in its actions under other provisions of the Treaty, in particular in order to respect and promote the diversity of its cultures.[3]

An important context in which such "taking into account" can occur, of course, is that of environmental impact review. EU policy for such review—both environmental impact assessment (EIA) on individual projects and programs and strategic environmental assessment (SEA) on policies and their implementation—is evolving rapidly. Cultural heritage—including not only "areas or features of historic or cultural importance" but also "cultural identity or associations"—is among the environmental elements upon which impacts are supposed to be analyzed under current procedures.[4]

The EIA/SEA procedures also provide for consultation as an important element of impact assessment and resolution, though (like NEPA in the United States) they tend to emphasize consultation with "authorities." With luck, democratic rather than authoritarian impulses will drive the evolution of the EU's environmental impact consultation policies toward consulting *everybody*, without giving anybody a veto.

Thus the EU has a legal basis for a broad, flexible, consultation-based program of cultural impact analysis, which I think would be much preferable to current practice, such as it is, in the United States.

The EU's emphasis on SEA—something that U.S. authorities talk about but haven't gone far toward implementing—presents some particularly interesting possibilities. The idea of SEA is to back up and look at environmental effects in the broadest possible contexts—geographic, temporal, and political. In SEA, the primary focus of evaluation is *policy*, rather than project. Is the tax system likely to drive family fishermen out of business, and is family fishing something that fishing communities or others value? What can be done about it? Do the fishermen or others want to preserve family fishing? Or should we accept its loss and look for ways to record and commemorate it? Is trade policy causing archeological sites to be plowed under to open more land for cultivation or auto works construction? What can be done to adjust the policy or to ratchet up the effectiveness of existing programs for identifying, preserving, and where necessary excavating sites? Cultural SEA will require sophisticated research, and consultation about it won't be easy. It's often difficult for people to anticipate the effects of policy; they become apparent only after they've begun to happen. But SEA holds great promise for avoiding last-minute conflicts and losing fights over the specific impacts of projects on heritage; it deserves a good deal of attention, and it appears that in Europe it may get it.

I imagine that there are strong conservative elements at work in the EU, however, that view "cultural heritage" as a thing of stones and dirt, of buildings and artwork, of landscapes and streetscapes, and that think of such heritage as something to be protected forever through government management. Such tendencies are likely to be strongest among professional cultural heritage managers, just as they are in the United States. The EU's need to assuage the justified fears of its nations and citizens about loss of cultural identity will not be served by maintaining such conservative assumptions and authoritarian institutions, but no doubt many EU politicians assume they ought to leave culture to the "experts." So here's one more recommendation: *don't*. The experts—archaeologists, architectural historians, conservators, administrators of cultural ministries—are the products of their narrow disciplinary training and bureaucratic experience. Use their expertise where it's relevant, but don't kowtow to them, and *don't put them in charge*. Keep your eye on the goal of a fair deal for the diverse cultural values of all Europeans, and make sure the "experts" are supervised by real people.

Conclusion: Back in the USA

OK, let's come back across the sea and apply what I've suggested for the EU to Mitch's original request—that I outline what I think ought to be done with the U.S. CRM system.

It's really pretty simple. I think we should:

- Reduce the status of the National Register; make it a list of those places in whose physical preservation people have invested or are ready to invest.

- Recognize the cultural environment—the world of cultural resources—as a very broad one, in which intangible beliefs, values, and perceptions are the key resources, sometimes but not always expressed in physical places and things. Don't require that such resources—physical or not—be listed or located on the ground, or that they be accorded significance in perpetuity; just provide for them to be respected in planning and policy.

- Require broad consultation with stakeholders about how to manage the cultural environment writ large in the course of land use and program planning and in the context of specific project planning. Do this by effectively combining the strengths of NEPA and Section 106 while discarding their weaknesses. Make sure that consultation includes everyone who has cultural concerns about an area, a program, a resource or resource type, and that the goal of consultation is to reach and memorialize (and then implement) binding agreements. Where agreement cannot be reached, provide for the responsible agency to make a decision after a thorough weighing of the impacts and alternative proposals for their resolution.

- Analyze impacts, and consult, not only about projects and programs with specific geographical scope, but about broad programs and policies too. Use consultation-based SEA to identify and try to resolve culture/development conflicts before they become intractable.

Put these together, and chuck the bureaucratic baggage with which what passes for a U.S. CRM system has burdened itself, and I think one could have a good, responsible, balanced program. Given the choice of betting that such reform will ever take place in the United States and betting that something of the sort might be taken up by the EU, however, I think I'd put my money on the Europeans.

177

Notes

1. UNESCO 1998.
2. See Fisher, Ury, and Patton 1991.
3. European Union 1993: Article 151 point 4.
4. European Commission 1985.

Glossary

ACHP ("Advisory Council"; "Council"): Advisory Council on Historic Preservation. A small, independent U.S. government agency that advises the president and Congress on historic preservation matters and oversees the Section 106 process (see below).

ACRA: American Cultural Resources Association. A trade organization of CRM companies and practitioners (mostly but not entirely archeologists), whose Internet forum "ACRA-L" is one of the few places where one can find actual CRM issues freely debated.

AIRFA: American Indian Religious Freedom Act. A joint resolution of Congress establishing it as U.S. government policy to protect Indian tribal rights to the free exercise of traditional religions.

CEQ: Council on Environmental Quality. An element of the Executive Office of the President, which is the president's general advisor on environmental matters and which oversees compliance with NEPA (see below).

CFR: Code of Federal Regulations. Regulations are cited by Title (the numbers preceding the "CFR") and Part or Section (the numbers following). Thus the regulations that agencies are supposed to follow in complying with the National Environmental Policy Act are 40 CFR 1500–1508 (Title 40, Sections 1500–1508 of the Code); those to be followed in complying with section 106 of the National Historic Preservation Act are 36 CFR 800 (Title 36, Part 800 of the Code).

CRM: "Cultural Resource Management." A catch-all euphemism for what people do to manage things of cultural value or impacts on such things. Different people understand it to mean different things. Archeologists, who invented the term in the early 1970s, typically understand it to mean doing archeology with the public's money. Museum people understand it to mean conserving museum specimens. Architectural historians understand it as a synonym for "historic preservation." I try to promote a broad but grounded definition, as the management of all culturally valued aspects of the physical and social environment and of the impacts that they experience as the results of development and change.[1]

HABS/HAER: The Historic American Buildings Survey/Historic American Engineering Record. A division of the National Park Service (NPS) that records historic buildings and engineering facilities and processes.

Historic preservation: The management of "historic properties" and impacts upon them. U.S. government agencies do historic preservation primarily under the authority of NHPA.

Historic property: In U.S. government parlance, any "district, site, building, structure, or object" that is included in or eligible for the National Register of Historic Places (National Register)—a list of known significant properties maintained by the National Park Service (NPS).

Indian tribe: Technically, a tribal government officially recognized or acknowledged as such by the U.S. government. Federally recognized tribes are domestic dependent sovereign nations, toward which the U.S. government is supposed to exercise a "trust" responsibility. Many have specific rights reserved under treaties, which are supposed to be the supreme law of the land. More generally, the term is also used to refer to groups that really or probably are historical/cultural tribes that have never gotten recognized by the federal government or that have had such recognition stripped away during one of that government's periodic fits of assimilation.

Keeper: The Keeper of the National Register. The NPS official who oversees the National Register of Historic Places and the NPS division that maintains it. The name was deliberately chosen by the founders of the national historic preservation program to spread a sort of old-world, monastic aura over the title holder.

NAGPRA: Native American Graves Protection and Repatriation Act. This statute provides for the repatriation of ancestral remains and "Native American cultural items" to tribes and Native Hawaiian groups, via a complex process of identification, validation of title, and consultation prescribed in NPS regulations (43 CFR 10).

National Register: The National Register of Historic Places. A list of districts, sites, buildings, structures, and objects that have been formally evaluated and found to be significant in American history, architecture, archeology, engineering, or culture, at national, state, or local levels of significance. The Register is maintained by NPS, and added to by nominations from agencies, states, Indian tribes, local governments, and the public. The same term is used for the NPS division that maintains the Register.

National Trust: The National Trust for Historic Preservation in the United States. Modeled on the like-named organization in Great Britain, the National Trust is a congressionally chartered membership organization that promotes historic preservation and manages a number of historic properties around the nation. It is the major (if not always the most effective) national advocate for historic preservation.

NCPE: National Council for Preservation Education. A national organization of graduate and undergraduate educational programs in historic preservation.

NEPA: National Environmental Policy Act. The statute that establishes overall U.S. government policy toward the environment and that specifically requires the assessment of federal agency actions on the environment.

NHPA: National Historic Preservation Act. The statute that defines the overall U.S. national historic preservation program, including such institutions as the ACHP, the National Register, and Section 106 review.

NPS: National Park Service. It counts among its "external programs" (i.e., programs not carried out primarily by, in, or for units of the National Park System) many aspects of the national historic preservation program, including the National Register and a number of professional standard-setting functions.

Section 106: Section 106 of the National Historic Preservation Act (NHPA), the core legal requirement upon which the U.S. national historic preservation program is built. Section 106 requires federal agencies to "take into account" the effects of their actions on "historic properties," and to afford the ACHP a reasonable opportunity to comment on such actions. Impact assessment under Section 106 and its regulations (36 CFR 800) is referred to as the "Section 106 process," or "Section 106 review."

Section 110: Another section of NHPA, which establishes a broad range of more or less unregulated federal agency responsibilities vis-à-vis historic preservation—including maintaining historic properties under agency authority, consulting about impacts on such properties, giving priority to the use of historic properties to meet mission requirements, discouraging the destruction and encouraging the preservation of nonfederally owned properties, and so on.

Bibliography

ACHP (Advisory Council on Historic Preservation)
  1988a Policy Statement Regarding Treatment of Human Remains and Grave Goods, adopted by the Advisory Council on Historic Preservation September 27, 1988, Gallup, New Mexico.
  1988b Advisory Council Policy Interpretation Memorandum 89–1, "Treatment of Human Remains and Grave Goods," issued December 1, 1988.
  2000 Protection of Historic Properties. 36 CFR 800.

Crespi, Muriel (Miki)
  2001 Raising Muted Voices and Identifying Invisible Resources. *CRM* 23:5:4–6, 2001.

Cummings, Calvin
  1983 "A Matter of Ethics," Introduction to The Proceedings of the Fourteenth Annual Conference on Underwater Archaeology. Council on Underwater Archaeology, Denver.

Dewdney, Selwyn
  1975 *The Sacred Scrolls of the Southern Ojibway*. Glenbow-Alberta Institute, Calgary, Alberta; University of Toronto Press, Toronto.

Ellen, R.F., ed.
  1984 *Ethnographic Research: A Guide to General Conduct*. Academic Press, London, Orlando, San Diego.

BIBLIOGRAPHY

European Commission
  1985   Directive 85/337/EEC: Assessment of the Effects of Certain Public
         and Private Projects on the Environment (as amended by Directive
         97/11/EC).

European Union
  1993   Treaty on European Union (the Maastricht Treaty), as amended.

Fisher, Roger, William Ury, and Bruce Patton
  1991   *Getting to Yes: Negotiating Agreement Without Giving In.* Second Edi-
         tion, Penguin Books, New York.

Freeman, Larry
  1992   *How to Write Quality EISs and EAs.* Shipley Associates, Bountiful,
         Utah.

Hamilton, Christopher E.
  1988   Reply to the Executive Committee, SHA, Concerning the Presentation
         of the Paper "Results of Archaeological Testing at WFL-HA-1, the
         Whydah Site." ms. Submitted to the Society for Historical Archaeol-
         ogy.

Interorganizational Committee on Guidelines and Principles for Social Impact
  Assessment
  1994   Guidelines and Principles for Social Impact Assessment. *Environmen-
         tal Impact Assessment Review* 15:1:11–44.

Juergensmeyer, Mark
  2000   *Terror in the Mind of God: The Global Rise of Religious Violence.* Univer-
         sity of California Press, Berkeley.

King, Thomas F.
  1998a *Cultural Resource Laws and Practice: An Introductory Guide.* AltaMira
         Press, Walnut Creek, Calif.
  1998b How the Archaeologists Stole Culture. A Gap in American Environ-
         mental Impact Assessment and What to Do about It. *Environmental
         Impact Assessment Review,* January 1998.
  1999   *In the Light of the Megis: Chequemogon Bay as a Traditional Cultural
         Property.* Report submitted to the Bad River and Red Cliff Bands of
         Lake Superior Chippewa.
  2000   *Federal Planning and Historic Places: The Section 106 Process.* AltaMira
         Press, Walnut Creek, Calif.

King, Thomas F., and Ethan Rafuse
    1994 NEPA and the Cultural Environment: an Assessment and Recommen-
          dations. Study prepared for Council on Environmental Quality by
          CEHP, Inc., Washington D.C., under Order No. EO 4005.

King, Thomas F., Randall Jacobson, Karen R. Burns, and Kenton Spading
    2001 *Amelia Earhart's Shoes.* AltaMira Press, Walnut Creek, Calif.

Lipe, W. D., and A. J. Lindsay
    1974 *Proceedings of the 1974 Cultural Resource Management,* Conference
          Technical Series No.14, Museum of Northern Arizona, Flagstaff.

McCarthy, John P.
    1996 Who Owns These Bones? Descendant Communities and Partnerships
          in the Excavation and Analysis of Historic Cemetery Sites in New York
          and Philadelphia. *Public Archaeology Review* 4:2:3–12.

NPS (National Park Service)
    1981 National Register of Historic Places (Regulations); 36 CFR Part 60; 46
          FR 56183–95.
    1983 Secretary of the Interior's Standards for Identification. 48 Federal Reg-
          ister 44720–23, Washington, D.C.
    2001 *People and Places: The Ethnographic Connection.* CRM 23:5, Washing-
          ton, D.C.

Parker, P. L., and T. F King
    1990 *Guidelines for Evaluating and Documenting Traditional Cultural Properties,*
          National Register *Bulletin* 38, National Park Service, Washington, D.C.

Rathje, William, and Cullen Murphy
    2001 *Rubbish! The Archaeology of Garbage,* University of Arizona Press, Tucson.

Schuldenrein, Joseph
    1995 The Care and Feeding of Archaeologists: A Plea for Pragmatic Train-
          ing in the 21st Century. Society for American Archaeology *Bulletin,*
          June/July/August: 22–24.

Sullivan, Alan P. III, John A. Hanson, and Rebecca A. Hawkins
    1994 *CRM* 17:9:30, National Park Service.

Thomas, David H.
    1975 Nonsite Sampling in Archaeology: Up the Creek Without a Site. In
          Sampling in Archaeology, edited by J. W. Mueller, pp. 45–60. University
          of Arizona Press, Tucson.

2001 *Skull Wars: Kennewick Man, Archaeology, and the Battle for Native American Identity.* Basic Books, New York.

Time
1995 Don't Tread on Me: An Inside Look at the West's Growing Rebellion. Time 146:17:62, 66, October 23.

UNESCO
1998 First Framework Programme in Support of Culture (2000–2004), Commission of the European Communities, Brussels.

U.S. Conference of Mayors
1967 *With Heritage So Rich.* Random House, New York.

Index

American Anthropological
Association, 14n9
American Association of State
Highway and Transportation
Officials, 76
American Cultural Resources
Association (ACRA): ix, 179
American Indian Movement, 105
American Indian Religious Freedom
Act, 8, 139, 179; and traditional
cultural properties, 113, 115
American Indians Against
Desecration (AIAD), 105
American Psychological Association,
14n9
American Sociological Association,
14n9
Anasazi pots, 168
ancestors: respect for, 106–11
ancestral village sites vs. archeological
sites, 17
Antiquities Act, 147
APE. *See* area of potential effects
applicants for federal assistance and
permits, 54, 60–73
"archeo-bias," 147–53; guarding
against, 151–53; symptoms, 150–51
Archeological Conservancy, 164, 169
Archeological Data Preservation Act
(ADPA), 147
Archeological and Historic
Preservation Act (AHPA), 147
Archeological Resource Protection
Act (ARPA), 147, 166
archeological sites: "100 percent
survey" to find, 124–25; data
recovery as mitigating impacts on,
123, 143; definitions of, 166;
immunity to visual impacts, 71;
integrity of, 154–63; "pedestrian

survey" to find, 149–50; physical
avoidance as mitigating impacts on,
123; vs. ancestral village sites, 17
archeologists and archeology:
distortion of CRM by, 6–13,
147–53; dominance of CRM by,
5–8, 145–46; ethical standards of,
165; interpretations of integrity,
154–63; "New," 156; and the
public, 26–29; "Settlement," 156
"archeo-talk," 123–25
architectural surveys: when
appropriate in visual impact cases,
72; windshield, 148
area of potential effects: definition,
128n8; mis-equated by
archeologists with project area,
149–52; for visual impacts, 70–73
Arkansas, 149
ARPA. *See* Archeological Resources
Protection Act
artifacts, ethics of selling, 164–69
Aten, Lawrence, 13n3
Atlantis, 170

Banker, Sherman, 73n10
"beyond impact assessment" ("beyond
106") concept: naivete of, 35
BLM. *See* Bureau of Land
Management
Bonanza Coin and Stamp, 164
Bordeaux vintners, 171
Bureau of Indian Affairs, 114
Bureau of Land Management
(BLM), 29n2, 74n3, 114
Bureau of Reclamation, 129

CEHP, Inc., 8
CEQ. *See* Council on Environmental
Quality

"potential" eligibility for National Register, 65–69

pothunter, xiii; defined, xixn3

preservation: disciplines, 33; vs. process, 31–34; *uber alles,* 31

principled negotiation, 135

process: vs. preservation, 31–34; Section 106 (*see* Section 106); transformation, 158–59

"professionalism," 22–23, 27

Program alternatives under Section 106, 84

Programmatic Agreement, 52, 84

Programmatic Memorandum of Agreement (PMOA), 52

Public: Shut out of Section 106 review, 54

Pyrenees, 174

Rafuse, Nathan, 13n5

Rathje, William, 166

reburial vs. repatriation of human remains and grave goods, 104–11

Republicans, seizure of Congress by in 1994, 48

"the resource": archeological, as defined by ARPA, 166; balanced consideration of, 33; expected advocacy of by CRM practitioners, 21; misplaced focus on, 72; perceived paramountcy, 31

Rural Sociology Society, 14n9

SAA. *See* Society for American Archaeology

Saratoga Battlefield, 73

Schuldenrein, Joseph, 13n2

Schwabacher Site, 155

SEA. *See* Strategic Environmental Assessment

Sebastian, Lynne, 120–22, 140

Secretary of the Interior, xii; *Standards for Identification,* 142

Section 106 (of NHPA): as centerpiece of U.S. national historic preservation program, 24; contrasting understandings of, 38–47; criteria of adverse effect, 72; delegation of duties under, 96; defined, 181; documentation requirements and suggestions, 86–96; evaluating properties under, 41–42, 91–92; identifying properties under, 40–41; initiating review under, 39–40, 88–90; Memorandum of Agreement under, based on flexible consultation, 141; mitigation under, 43–44; "no adverse effect"determinations under, 93–95; "no historic properties subject to effect" determinations under, 92–93; perceived rigidity of, 70–73; purpose, 51; regulatory requirements outlined, 38–47; resolving adverse effects under, 43; scoping under, 88–90; and Section 4(f) of DOT Act, 76–80; substituting NEPA for standard process of, 95–96; threshold for review, 81; what's wrong with it, 52–58

September 11, 2001, xvi

Shipley Associates, 13n6

SHPO. *See* State Historic Preservation Officer

SIA. *See* Social Impact Assessment

Significance: assigned, not intrinsic, 172

Silver Spring, Maryland, 164

Social Impact Assessment (SIA), 1; Guidelines and Principles of, 12–13, 14n10

About the Author

om King began working in cultural resource management at the age of ten, when he pulled up a housing developer's survey stakes on his family chicken ranch in California and tossed them over the fence. Like many of his subsequent attempts to control the impacts of change, this one proved futile. King went on to be a teenaged pothunter (i.e., an illicit excavator of archeological sites), a salvage archeologist (i.e., a licit excavator of such sites in the teeth of their destruction), and the head of university archeological field programs in California before (a) completing his Ph.D. and (b) irritating people sufficiently that he was run out of the state. He subsequently worked for the New York Archaeological Council, the National Park Service, the Trust Territory of the Pacific Islands, and the Advisory Council on Historic Preservation before wearing out his welcome in government and going into private practice. Since 1989 he has worked as a consultant, teacher, writer, facilitator, and sometimes mediator, trying to help people understand and cope with the nation's cultural resource laws and procedures. He teaches short courses for the National Preservation Institute (www.npi.org) and continues an avocational interest in archaeology in The International Group for Historic Aircraft Recovery's (www.tighar.org) pursuit of Amelia Earhart across the central Pacific.

In the course of his career King has worked with Indian tribes, Micronesian communities, federal and state agencies, local governments, regulated utilities, consulting firms, community organizations, and international groups. He has published three textbooks and many journal articles, monographs, government regulations and guidelines, and contributions to the gray literatures of historic preservation, archaeology, environmental impact assessment, and other fields. He is particularly known for his work with "traditional cultural properties"—places whose cultural significance lies in the minds of local communities rather than or as well as in the minds of "experts." His coauthored (with Patricia L. Parker) "Identification and Documentation of Traditional Cultural Properties" (National Register *Bulletin* 38; National Park Service 1990) is especially notorious.

AltaMira Press offers the following King publications:

Cultural Resource Laws and Practice: An Introductory Guide (1998)
Federal Planning and Historic Places: The Section 106 Process (2000)
Amelia Earhart's Shoes: Is the Mystery Solved? (2001)
A book on traditional cultural properties is forthcoming in 2003.

To communicate with King about this book or other CRM matters, email tfking106@aol.com.